Protecting Restaurant Profits: Managing Security

Stephen G. Miller

Protecting Restaurant Profits: Managing Security

Stephen G. Miller

Lebhar Friedman Books
Chain Store Publishing Corp.
A Subsidiary of Lebhar Friedman, Inc.
New York

Prepared for

The Educational Foundation of the National Restaurant Association Foodservice Manager Self-Development Program

Protecting Restaurant Profits: Managing Security

10 9 8 7 6 5 4 3 2 1

Printed in the United States of America
Library of Congress Catalog Card Number: 87-073516
International Standard Book Number: 086730-252-6

Introduction

Protecting Restaurant Profits: Managing Security is divided into two parts. Part I, Internal Control, covers internal theft in restaurants while Part II, The External Dimension, discusses external threats to restaurant security.

Part I, chapters 1 through 8, provides an understanding of employee theft and a strong, practical control tool for preventing it. These chapters explain why managers must be aware of the nature and extent of employee theft, the conditions which encourage it, and the steps necessary to implement an effective theft-prevention program.

The first step for managers in preventing employee theft is to recognize that a problem could exist and to accept responsibility for on-site conduct of their employees. Unfortunately, many managers ignore what they consider an unpleasant task until an incident occurs. If individual incidents are not dealt with directly, the situation becomes corrosive, with more and more employees joining in theft from the employer.

Understanding employees—what motivates them, their need for self-esteem, and relating to that need—is the manager's next step in employee theft control. If managers know why employees steal and which preventive methods are most effective, they will be better able to formulate a theft deterrent and control plan. For example, many managers incorrectly believe that employee theft is a personal assault; actually, most employees who steal think they are stealing from an impersonal company "that can take a little loss." Along the same lines, many employees don't regard what they are doing as "stealing" at all.

Throughout Part I the importance of management ideals and the manager's concern for employees is emphasized. One trend which tends to increase internal crime today is the trend toward absentee owners and its failure to foster employee loyalty. Caring for employees as individuals is necessary to the manager-employee relationship. Statistics can point out realities, theft-prevention programs can establish guidelines and procedures, but a healthy working climate is the bottom line in theft prevention. Motivation and morale are the most important factors in building an optimum climate. Part I discusses these factors and suggests ways managers can improve them.

INTRODUCTION

Part II focuses on external threats to restaurant security. These include robbery, burglary, fraud, forgery, larceny, vandalism, and extortion. Security specialists estimate that 25 to 50 percent of a restaurant's losses results from these types of crimes. Although these represent a smaller proportion of loss than internal crimes, external crimes cause monetary loss and difficult, emotional—sometimes dangerous—situations for both employees and guests.

To cut down on such losses and effectively handle situations involving safety risks, restaurateurs must understand the nature of external crimes and of the criminals who perpetrate them. Managers must also be aware of crime prevention techniques, pertinent laws, and their companies' safety and security policies and procedures.

Chapters 9 through 11 define the various types of external threats, present common prevention techniques, and give other general advice on reducing external problems in restaurants.

Preface

Protecting Restaurant Profits: Managing Security updates and comple-
ments Bob Curtis' best-selling trade books *Food Service Security: Internal
Control* and *Security Control: External Theft* to give restaurant operators,
managers, and security personnel a comprehensive body of work on
preventing profit losses.

Since the publication of the original books, the focus of restaurant
security programs has shifted, and loss-prevention techniques have
now become more sophisticated.

The premise of the original internal control work was that managers could prevent internal crimes by establishing quality relationships
with their employees and by setting up a positive work climate. Although these are still important elements of an effective internal security program, today's restaurant security experts believe two other
elements are equally important: 1) communicating to employees that
theft will not be tolerated; and 2) separating the cash handling, accounting, and auditing responsibilities of employees. In terms of external thefts, experts believe new deterrents are needed to combat the
increasing number of crimes against restaurants.

This text explains how restaurateurs can set up modern security
programs which address these internal and external changes, and its
presents model policies and procedures which, when implemented, are
proven crime deterrents.

This book can stand alone as an introductory text on restaurant
security, or can form part of a Self-Development course sponsored by
the Educational Foundation of the National Restaurant Association.

As consulting author on this text, I would like to thank those
restaurant professionals whose guidance and cooperation have been
invaluable to me in gathering up-to-date restaurant security information:

- William P. Fisher, Ph.D., Executive Vice President, and Richard
  J. Gaven, Senior Director, of the National Restaurant Association.

- Dick Moe, Tom Briggs, Lee Winkler, Frank Barnaby, Emil
  Monda, and all the other members of the Foodservice Security
  Council.

- Robert A. Beck, Jack E. Miller, and Donald I. Smith, colleagues and friends.

Hopefully, the information presented in this text will help industry operators and managers develop effective security programs that will curb crime and protect profits.

Contents

Part I
Internal Control

An Overview

Dimensions of the Problem

Internal theft is a major problem facing the nation's businesses. It is "the unauthorized taking, control, or transfer of money and/or property of the formal work organization that is perpetrated by an employee during the course of occupational activity." (5) Because of internal theft, businesses lose between 5 and 10 billion dollars each year. (4)

The restaurant industry is especially susceptible to such losses because: (1, 3)

- Employees have access to cash.

- There is high employee turnover.

- Internal control systems are often inadequate, especially in smaller operations.

- Expensive items, such as liquor and meats, are highly desirable.

- It is possible to combine house receipts with tips.

- Theft can be ascribed to waste since so many products are perishable.

- Low wage structure can lead to unauthorized "raises."

"Five cents of every dollar a restaurant rings up in sales are lost to theft. Out of that nickel, four cents are pocketed by the restaurant's employees." (2) Internal theft accounts for about 75 percent of a restaurant's inventory shortages, while paperwork errors and external losses account for the rest. One industry study showed that one-third of employees surveyed "reported some involvement in the taking of company property . . . during the prior year." (5)

Employee thefts multiply losses well beyond the specific amounts stolen. Although restaurateurs consider losses in terms of percentage of sales, they are actually related directly to profits. A restaurant with a 3 percent net profit that suffers a 1 percent cash shortage has actually lost more than one-third of its profits. The restaurant has lost the profits on the food it must sell to pay for this shortage. Some restaurants must set aside a percentage of sales as a reserve or operate without a profit for a period in order to cover their internal losses.

Serious Consequences

Besides the damage to profits, internal theft results in other costly consequences:

- The loss of employees whom the restaurant has trained.

- Heavy costs in training employees to replace those dismissed.

- A lowering of morale throughout the restaurant when an employee who had been considered honest and valuable is suspect.

- Other employees use the example of dishonest co-workers to justify their own thefts.

- Possible loss of important and irreplaceable records through theft.

- Bad publicity which can damage a restaurant's image.

In emotional as well as financial terms, thefts cause loss and damage to both individuals and businesses.

Almost unconsciously, many restaurant executives think of employee dishonesty as part of the routine cost of doing business. They may admit they do not know how much theft loss their companies suffer each year. Even when they acknowledge that some losses occur, they may show little interest in exploring the matter.

Employers can inadvertently be accomplices to dishonest employees. If employers do not project an attitude that fosters proper behavior, employees may very well develop the employer's lax view. Employees may not regard stealing from their employers as theft and do not consider themselves thieves. This unconscious collusion between employer and employee sanctions and perpetuates internal theft.

Influence of the Work Environment

In a three-year study of employee theft, the National Institute of Justice (NIJ) found that, in addition to the one-third of employees who "reported stealing company property . . . two-thirds reported misconduct such as sick leave abuse, drug or alcohol use on the job, and falsifying time sheets." (5) The NIJ suggests that employee theft of money or property not be viewed in isolation, but rather as one manifestation of "employee deviance." Causes—and cures—should be sought in the work environment itself, not in an individual employee's character or circumstances or in the local crime rate.

The NIJ report states, "Perceived honesty and fairness of the organization" influence employee behavior more than security controls. The study warns that the control of property theft "might easily lead to the burgeoning of other acts against the production norms of the organization . . . if the underlying causes of employee deviance have not been addressed." (5)

What factors influence an employee's view of the organization? The NIJ cites five:

- Competence of supervisors.

- Adequacy of communication.

- Fairness in employer-employee relations.

- Employer recognition of quality performance.

- Ethical behavior by higher management.

The report also recommends developing career potential for all employees because "blocked channels of opportunity" may result in theft or counter-productive behavior. Much of the trustworthiness of a restaurant's staff is due directly to the quality of the relationships between the restaurant managers and their employees. "Employees can and should be made to feel that it's their company; people don't steal from themselves. Participative management . . . is sound security policy." (5)

Need for Controls

A controlled working environment and firm policies ensure employee honesty. To be productive, employees need to feel emotionally secure on the job. Lack of controls breeds insecurity.

One of the most effective ways to inhibit internal theft is to let employees know that theft will not be tolerated and to back that up with swift enforcement.

Restaurants should have a code of ethics, a "clearly defined and promulgated anti-theft policy." (5) Regulations should provide specifics for the handling of food, money, and other property. Employees must be told of the requirements at their entry interviews, and copies of the regulations should be posted prominently.

The three main restaurant control functions—cash handling, accounting, and inventory control—must be handled by different people to minimize potential losses and make problems and inconsistencies apparent sooner. Dividing duties wherever possible creates a system of checks and balances all along the line.

Management's Role

When employees steal, the consequences are painful for both restaurant operators and employees. Accusations can harm individuals and their families. Even questioning an individual may imply guilt. Confronting a trusted employee with a charge of dishonesty or theft is not a pleasant task. Moreover, it is a task that can be avoided by using the proper preventive measures.

It is the restaurant operator's responsibility to make sure that temptations to steal are not realized. This can be done by setting up systems to combat internal theft and by implementing methods to keep employees honest. Good management skills, careful personnel screening, high employee morale, and careful planning to avert potential problems—all contribute to success in this area. "Work place deviance is in large part a reflection of how management at all levels is perceived by the employee, and a management team that is responsible to the perceptions, attitudes, and needs of its work force may well expect to experience a decrease in the incidence of deviant behavior." (5)

1

The Way to Begin: Screening Employees

The Importance of Screening

The applicant for the "Assistant Manager" position seemed to have all the qualities the restaurant owners wanted. The applicant had the right reasons for wanting to change jobs and sound goals for the new position. The owners were convinced of the applicant's ability and potential. Rather than waste time checking the applicant's background, they decided to have the applicant take a polygraph test. The applicant took the test, passed it, and was hired immediately.

It wasn't long after the employee had been on the job that the owners noticed shortages of both cash and food items in the restaurant. Since they couldn't account for the losses from any external source, they began to investigate possible internal sources of the thefts, including checking the new assistant manager's background and references. To their dismay, they discovered that the new employee had false references and numerous convictions for theft.

7

Hiring this assistant manager had two consequences for the restaurant: profit loss due to the employee's thefts, and decreased morale among the staff who were aware that the assistant manager was stealing and resented being supervised by a thief.

How could this have happened? It happened because the owners relied on their intuition and a polygraph test rather than on sound policies and procedures for employee screening. Intuition and polygraphs may be useful in some instances, but are far from foolproof hiring tools.

The experience of these owners is not unique. After a thief has been apprehended, employers often discover that there was negative preemployment information on the person that had been overlooked or disregarded.

Components of Employment Screening

Employment screening involves checking an applicant's background as carefully and completely as possible prior to hiring, to be reasonably sure the applicant is honest and right for the job. Screeners use a variety of tools, such as applications, background and reference checks, and interviews, to gather facts about applicants in accordance with federal and state laws. They then have the responsibility to interpret this data to help them make hiring decisions.

Companies have various policies for designating which of their employees have screening responsibilities. In some companies, all screening is done centrally at headquarters by personnel or other types of executives; in others, owners, managers, or other designated employees at the facility have the responsibility. Those who are assigned the screening function must have the expertise and be given time to do the job correctly.

Over the years, experts have developed screening tools that help in assessing the quality and honesty of job applicants. These tools require a bit of knowledge and effort to master, but they do help reduce internal theft.

Employment Applications: A Critical Tool

Whether restaurants are large or small, a written job application is a must. An application introduces an applicant to a screener and serves as a starting point for judging the applicant's merits. Basic application information includes: an applicant's name, address, telephone number, social security number, educational background, and work experiences; names, addresses, and telephone numbers of references; and other information the restaurant deems necessary.

Federal and state regulations limit what type of questions an applicant can be asked. Employers *cannot* ask applicants questions concerning race, marital status, religious affiliation, or ethnicity. Nor can employers ask questions concerning: (1)

- **Birth date or age, unless such information is needed to fulfill the legal requirements of a position.** Upon hiring, they can ask minors to produce working papers or employees who would need to serve alcoholic beverages to produce proof of age.

- **Place of birth.** Employers may not inquire about the birthplace of the applicant or of members of the applicant's family.

- **National origin or ancestry.** Employers cannot ask questions concerning the ancestry, lineage, nationality, national origin, parentage, or descent of applicants or their family members.

- **How citizenship was acquired.** Employers may ask if applicants are U.S. citizens or if they can legally work in the United States. However, they cannot ask applicants whether they are native-born or naturalized citizens. After employment, according to the Immigration Reform and Control Act of 1986, employers must request and examine documentation of identity and employment eligibility.

- **Maiden name.** Requesting a maiden name, or a spouse's name or maiden name, is prohibited.

- **Number and age of children or child-bearing plans when there are no children.** Also, employers cannot ask applicants what provisions they have for childcare.

- **Physical disabilities.** "Discrimination against the physically handicapped is unlawful if the applicant is able and competent to perform the duties of the job. Employing units should be aware that they are under an obligation to take affirmative action to employ and promote qualified handicapped and disabled veteran employees, including an obligation to make reasonable accommodations for handicapped employees under Department of Labor Regulations issued pursuant to the Vocational Rehabilitation Act of 1973 and Vietnam Era Veteran Readjustment

Assistance Act of 1974." (1) Note that this act has been broadly interpreted to include alcoholics and drug addicts as "handicapped workers."

- **Civic, religious, or fraternal organizational memberships.** Employers are only permitted to ask about membership in organizations which are not indicative of race, religion, color, sex, national origin, or ancestry.

- **Arrest history.** Employers may ask applicants if they have been convicted of a crime, but not if they have ever been arrested.

Screeners examine job applications to determine what they reveal about applicants. Incomplete applications, overly amended forms (e.g., erasures, cross-outs, etc.), gaps in dates of employment, and frequent job changes are indicative of potentially high-risk employees. When these occur, screeners need to ask applicants to explain them.

Background Checks

Effective screening entails checking the background of every job applicant. The depth of the background check depends on the position to be filled. The most extensive checking is done for positions in which employees handle large amounts of cash or have access to valuable merchandise (e.g., accountants, cashiers, wine stewards). Background checks can include verifying employment application information, obtaining and checking references, conducting police department checks, and looking for other evidence of past dishonesty.

Verifying Employment Application Information

When appropriate, screeners require applicants to submit factual materials which support the statements on their employment applications. These may include social security cards, drivers' licenses, high school equivalency papers, high school or college graduation records, and other written evidence.

Screeners must examine submitted materials to ensure they are genuine. Since social security cards, diplomas, drivers' licenses, and other forms of identification can be forged, screeners should be trained to detect signs of counterfeiting and use industry resources to keep their knowledge up-to-date. Many employers use the *I.D. Checking Guide* (available from the Driver's License Guide Company, 1492 Oddstad Drive, Redwood City, California 94063) to obtain information about drivers' licenses and related materials.

The Importance of References

Many in the restaurant industry question the value of having applicants list the names of references on their employment applications. They believe calling a person listed as a reference to ask questions about the applicant serves little purpose because the reply will be watered down by kindness, forgetfulness, negligence, or fear of committing oneself to a situation which may later prove embarrassing or illegal.

Despite the problems in getting useful, truthful replies, checking references does provide an impressive amount of vital data. A systematic reference check and a skillful analysis of the information it provides can help screeners evaluate an applicant's character, dependability, cooperativeness, level of productivity, and integrity. Moreover, applicants are less likely to give false information if they have heard that the restaurant always checks references.

Conducting a reference check by telephone and following the call with a written request is generally preferable to depending solely on correspondence. In a conversation, a screener can ask questions more informally and ask the reference giver to elaborate on answers when necessary. People giving references will often say what they will not write, particularly when they have negative feelings about an applicant.

Many employers instruct their managers to provide only basic information about previous employees—just to confirm dates of employment. Other companies are untruthful and give good references to avoid lawsuits and potential unemployment costs. The most important question of all in checking with an applicant's previous employer is, "Would you rehire this person?" An answer to this question is almost always revealing.

During reference checks, interviewers may discover that applicants have lied about their past job experiences. They may never have worked for a particular firm, or a firm may be nonexistent. Uncovering such facts provides insights as to whether or not an applicant would be a suitable employee.

Screeners should attempt to contact all the companies for which an applicant has worked. It is necessary to cover a sufficient time span to obtain the complete pattern of an applicant's behavior. High school guidance counselors can often provide valuable information regarding the applicant who is just entering the work force.

Reference givers should be people who have seen the applicant perform in a variety of situations. It is a good idea to seek information not only from the owners or managers of former establishments at which the applicant worked, but from other former supervisors, colleagues, or subordinates as well.

Screeners must evaluate not only the applicant, but also the credibility of the reference source. Reference givers should be asked to explain how they arrived at their conclusions about the employee's capabilities and performance. Do the reference givers seem objective? Do their standards seem too high or low?

A reference's usefulness depends on the quality of the reference giver's replies to questions. Screeners should be wary when reference givers are vague or subjective in answering their questions, especially when negative comments have been made. Reference checkers must try to determine if bias is a factor or if a personality clash may be responsible for a negative report.

Competent screeners use a checklist of questions to ensure that a reference check is properly conducted. These questions pertain to the applicant's:

- Dates of employment.

- Positions held.

- Job responsibilities.

- Salary.

- Level of integrity.

- Dependability.

- Level of initiative and ambition on job.

- Relationships with associates and supervisors and their opinion of applicant.

- Would former employer rehire applicant? If not, why not?

No matter how quickly a restaurateur needs a position to be filled, references should be checked *prior to* hiring. Doing so is the best way to avoid costly hiring mistakes.

Police Department Checks

In areas where it is legal, some restaurateurs check with the local police department to find out if job applicants have been convicted of any crimes. To do this, they provide the police with the full name of the applicant along with the person's address, social security number, and other information obtained from the employment application. In areas where operators cannot legally ask the police to check an applicant's record, some request the applicant to do so by taking an "inquiry form" to the police station. The police are requested to sign the form stating that the applicant has never been convicted of a crime, and the form is returned to the restaurant's employment office.

If the applicant has lived in various places during the past ten years, the police in each location may be contacted by letter.

Using Evidence of Past Dishonesty

A United States Supreme Court decision stipulates that employers cannot ask job applicants if they have ever been arrested. Since arrests are not proof of guilt, interviewers must only use evidence of convictions in their hiring decisions.

Even rejection on the basis of criminal convictions may soon be made unlawful. Courts and agencies appear to be heading toward a ruling that people cannot be denied jobs even if they have been convicted of a crime, assuming the convictions are for youthful offenses or "minor" crimes. If this legislation should become a reality, the definition of "minor" crimes will be an extremely important guide in screening job applicants.

Screeners must make legally acceptable efforts to check on a candidate's past record of behavior. They should not hire employees without first checking to see if they have been convicted for crimes, especially for crimes against property, such as shoplifting, automobile theft, burglary, and robbery. Employing people with such backgrounds must be carefully weighed. It is often unfair to the company as well as the applicants to place them in positions of temptation.

Is it possible for people with police records to be good risks? Could they have learned their lesson and "gone straight"? Unfortunately, the evidence is not encouraging. Studies by criminal psychologists, security specialists, and the federal government have shown that people who are arrested for various theft offenses often repeat their crimes.

The Justice Department reports, "About half of the inmates released from state prisons will return within 20 years, and 60 percent of these repeaters will be back by the end of the third year." (12)

These startling figures are evidence that most applicants who have previous convictions are poor employment risks. Even if applicants admit that they have stolen previously and have served prison terms, interviewers should not assume that these people are good risks because they have been truthful about their past. They may have admitted their past offenses because they felt interviewers would know of them, or discover them in background checks. Frankness about a previous criminal record should not be mistaken for integrity.

Interviewing Job Applicants

Screening does not reveal many of an applicant's characteristics. Employers need to conduct interviews with every job applicant to determine if they are suitable for a particular position. They assess whether applicants seem to have a positive outlook, enthusiasm and drive, the necessary knowledge, skills, and experience to do the job, maturity, persistence, tact, and integrity.

An interview also gives an employer the opportunity to determine whether an applicant's intelligence level is sufficient for the position. Some companies use intelligence tests, but most rely on intelligence-level indicators, such as an applicant's communication style, educational level attained, and ability to handle abstract concepts.

When evaluating an applicant's intelligence, interviewers should avoid pitfalls such as equating appearance with intelligence. The abilities of a good-looking, well-dressed person are often overrated, while those of a less attractive person are generally underrated. Surface appearances frequently mislead.

The Right Questions

Effective interviewers elicit information about an applicant's life such as education, military service (responsibilities), previous type of work, previous income, hobbies, personal interests, general health, and personal aspirations both on and off the job. Open-ended questions, which require more than a "yes" or "no" answer, are best because they give applicants a chance to express their views.

Interviewers engage applicants in conversations which reveal their feelings about the following: previous employment (including factors that might have motivated changes); personal stability and reliability; and general attitudes toward other subjects which arise in the interview. The quality of applicants' responses is critical. Do applicants agree with whatever is said in the conversation or do they state their opinions? Are questions answered logically, or emotionally?

Interviewers also need to assess an applicant's goals. Overly high aspirations for a job can lead to frustration on the job, a primary cause of theft.

Interviewers should also be alert to any indication of cheating or dishonesty on the part of the persons being questioned, particularly any contradictions or discrepancies in applicants' answers. Nothing should be taken for granted; interviewers need to be especially alert when applicants:

- Do not answer questions directly.

- Rationalize unfavorable reports, have glib explanations for gaps in their employment records, or talk too rapidly.
- Go into long and detailed descriptions of previous work experience and earnings.

Good questions are the key to a successful interview. An interviewer can ascertain an applicant's interests and abilities by asking questions such as:

- If you could create the perfect job for yourself, what would it be?
- In what jobs or capacities do you feel you have been most effective?
- What untapped resources do you feel you have that you could use in this job?
- What are your best qualities?
- What are your main character weaknesses?
- How do you react to criticism?
- Have you ever supervised the work of others? If so, how did you find the experience?
- How would you say you work with others?

Giveaway Gestures

Body language reveals a great deal about people. Interviewers should be sensitive to both verbal and nonverbal cues during the job interview and should try to determine why a particular topic elicits a specific reaction.

Using Tests

The screening tests discussed below are costly and time-consuming and are typically administered only to those applicants being considered for positions where they will be responsible for cash handling, accounting, or inventory control. Laws concerning the use of these tests vary. It is important that employers are aware of the laws in the locality of their facilities before adopting any of these tests.

Intelligence Tests

There is usually an optimum intelligence level for most jobs. Restaurateurs who use intelligence tests frequently test employees who have worked for them successfully for several years in order to determine what the optimum level is for their particular jobs. By identifying the intelligence levels of present employees, useful guidelines can be established for selecting individuals to fill the same or similar positions. From a security viewpoint, it is sound business practice to try to hire only those applicants who achieve at least the average level in the optimum intelligence standard set for each type of job. Applicants scoring considerably below the established level probably will be slow to learn the work and might not perform well. On the other hand, those who score considerably higher than the established level might become restless, bored, or frustrated. Although using intelligence tests is beneficial, they are not convenient to administer. Many employers prefer to determine the approximate range of an applicant's intelligence during an interview.

Honesty Tests

Honesty (or "paper and pencil" tests) are used by many companies. Some administer these tests themselves, while others hire consultants to give them. These tests contain questions about an applicant's past behavior and current attitudes toward theft. Many of these tests also have questions concerning the use of alcohol and illegal drugs. According to the developer of one honesty test, "There are significant differences in the way honest and dishonest people reply to certain questions. Each question has been chosen because of its ability to discriminately separate the people most likely to be honest from those who are likely to be profit-robbers." (5) For example, an honest person would answer the question, "Do you believe everyone is dishonest to a certain extent?" (11) differently than a dishonest person.

One honesty-test company reported that people identified as honest "by the test were considered generally more reliable, having a better work ethic, and being generally better individuals." (2) Others in the restaurant industry are less sure of the validity of these tests. Opponents of honesty tests feel that they are not accurate and cite that a person who fails the test once may know how to answer the questions when given the test a second time.

Polygraphs and Other Stress Measurements

Many restaurant managers say, "Why spend all this time and effort checking into people's backgrounds? We can give them a polygraph test and learn the whole story in an hour or two with much less trouble." In theory, relying on polygraphs seems appealing. Certainly, many companies who use them find them effective, particularly for obtaining the details of employee dishonesty after a crime has been uncovered. But their use in hiring raises some serious questions.

Some security experts feel that polygraphs represent an "easy way out" and are a poor substitute for a thorough interview and background check. Many people mistakenly believe that polygraphs are "lie detectors." Actually, a polygraph is a "stress detector that measures changes in perspiration, pulse rate, blood pressure, and/or breathing." (5) Therefore, a number of factors can cause a wrong diagnosis. These include illness, pain, coughing spells, mental or physical fatigue, heart conditions, hay fever, asthma, and use of certain medications. Even the manner in which the examiner acts toward the subject before the test can affect the results.

Although there are many extremely talented, well-trained, knowledgeable polygraph operators, there are others who are poorly trained, inexperienced, and lacking in the skills and understanding necessary to run reliable tests. It is imperative to engage the services of a true professional and avoid incompetent practitioners.

Through the efforts of the American Polygraph Association (APA) to establish a code of ethics and to monitor its members, the standards of professionalism in this field have risen steadily. Members of the APA have stringent education and training requirements which they must fulfill before they can practice. Because licensing requirements vary so greatly from state to state, any company considering the use of polygraph tests should make certain that the practitioner it uses has been accepted for membership in the APA.

Only a qualified operator has the training and experience to make a valid diagnosis. Unfortunately, irresponsible operators tend to mislead clients and often report passing or failing results when, in fact, they are not able to make a professional determination based on the polygraph evidence. Genuine polygraph experts can detect variables and work around them or reschedule tests, but untrained operators may be ignorant of these factors and may, therefore, deliver a false reading.

The legality and use of polygraphs are expected to remain controversial. Currently, Congress is considering two bills concerning the use of polygraphs. One bill would "prohibit employers from requiring, requesting, or suggesting that employees or prospective employees take a lie-detector test for any reason." (7) Pharmaceutical, nursing home, and day care workers are exempt from this ban, as are employees in positions that involve national security or classified information. (6)

The second bill allows employers to use polygraphs, but proposes standards for their use. (8) The National Restaurant Association (NRA) and many employers feel that polygraphs are useful tools and are opposed to banning their use. According to the NRA, if polygraphs are being misused, then the federal government "should adopt a licensing bill to professionalize polygraph examiners. The NRA also suggests that the bill earmark certain questions that cannot be used, such as questions that discriminate in hiring practices." (7)

Some security experts suggest that companies that use polygraphs to screen applicants also use them with their employees on a regular basis to maintain high standards of employee honesty over time. Others disagree. They believe giving periodic tests to employees is costly, time-consuming, and tends to set up a threatening work environment which actually fosters internal theft.

There are other forms of stress tests available, including voice-activated tests and psychological stress tests, but their use in the restaurant industry is limited.

Checking an Applicant's Financial Situation

In many companies, obtaining a credit bureau report on applicants who will handle cash or inventory is a part of the employment screening process. Restaurants use these reports to determine if applicants are under financial pressure because of large outstanding loans or other causes. They also reveal whether or not an applicant has recently been sued for nonpayment of debts or has had a garnishee.

If employers plan to check an applicant's credit history, they must comply with the Fair Credit Reporting Act. Credit bureaus cannot give out adverse information after three months without first verifying it to determine that it is still valid. Also, credit bureaus cannot report most legal proceedings against an individual after seven years, or bankruptcy proceedings after fourteen years. In addition to providing individuals with the right to know what is in their credit files, the Fair Credit Reporting Act provides regulations when others, including potential employers, want to learn about a person's credit history.

According to this Act, individuals must be notified in writing when this information is sought by others, and they have the right to know the type of information requested. Furthermore, if applicants are denied employment on the basis of what they consider to be incorrect information contained in the report, they have the right to challenge the information and provide the credit reporting agency with their version of the information. The credit agency must then pass along this information to the potential employer. (10)

Employers who use credit bureau reports often incorporate permission slips into their job applications for applicants to sign.

Bonding Company Forms

For positions in which employees have access to funds and valuable merchandise, many restaurants require that job applicants fill out a bonding company form in addition to the employment application. Applicants with criminal records are frequently concerned about bonding applications. They are aware that bonding companies investigate applicant's backgrounds and report criminal records to a restaurant. As a result, the use of bonding company forms is a theft deterrent. When they are used, many dishonest applicants do not return for a second interview.

Screening job applicants is a critical step in preventing internal theft in restaurants. But employers cannot be complacent about possible theft because they believe they have hired honest people. They must be alert to danger signs that employees have become high-risks to the company.

2
Employees Who Steal

Dishonesty's Warning Signs

One security expert believes, "If good security procedures are used in hiring employees, one must consider most employees to be honest when they begin employment with the company. Most people do not begin work with a company with the intention of stealing money or merchandise from the employer. The motivation or reasons to steal generally appear after the person has worked at his or her job for ... [some] time." (7)

How do employers determine which employees may become dishonest? They look for trouble-indicators such as:

- **Behavioral changes.** Employees who exhibit unpredictable behaviors, or who show other signs of emotional upset, are a cause for concern. Employers should be alert to employees who have been reliable and well-adjusted, but who suddenly become nervous, worried, withdrawn, hostile, or overly emotional in other ways.

- **Refusal to take a vacation.** Employees who refuse to take vacations may be afraid that substitutes who assume their positions while they are away would detect their dishonest acts.

- **Overprotection of work records or files.** Employees who are reluctant to give up custody of records or files or who always take them home may be keeping incriminating facts and documents close to them.

- **Overeagerness.** While conscientious employees are a plus, overly eager individuals who always rush into work early and leave late may be trying to create a hardworking, honest image to cover up their thefts.

- **Violating rules.** Employees who rebel against company policies and procedures should be watched. While misconduct (such as taking long lunch hours or breaks) is a form of employee theft, it may also indicate the employee is an outright thief.

- **Substance abuse.** Managers must know how to recognize signs of drug and alcohol abuse. Fair Oaks Hospital, a nationally prominent drug and alcohol treatment center, suggests employers watch for the warning signs listed in Chart 2.1.

- **Tattling.** When employees frequently turn in dishonest workers, they may actually be covering their own guilt by shifting blame to others.

- **Dishonest use of business contacts.** People who make dishonest demands upon vendors and other business contacts for unauthorized discounts or free items may be dishonest in other areas as well.

- **Frequent, heavy, or irresponsible borrowing.** Employees who frequently borrow large amounts of money may be driven to steal from any available source. They may borrow small amounts of money from co-workers and then fail to repay them. Their personal checks may be undated or postdated. Or, they may ask others not to cash their checks for a while.

- **Condoning dishonesty in others.** Employees who steal typically have different attitudes or beliefs than those who are honest. Instead of believing that theft is wrong, dishonest employees often condone the dishonesty of others. When employees in a company have been fired and prosecuted for theft, a typical response from a dishonest employee is, "I don't believe the

---

Chart 2.1. Warning Signs of Substance Abuse by Employees

- *Performance:*
  Lowered productivity.
  Poor concentration.
  Signs of fatigue.
  Increased mistakes.
  Sporadic work pace.
  Inconsistent work quality.

- *Attendance/absenteeism:*
  Increased lateness.
  Increased absenteeism.
  Vague complaints of illness.
  Stomach/intestinal distress, flu, headaches, sore throat, and sweating.
  Extended lunch periods or breaks.
  Complaints of personal and family problems.
  Unexplained disappearances from the workplace.

- *Attitude/appearance:*
  Mood swings.
  Borrowing money from friends or co-workers.
  Isolation.
  Radical loss or gain of weight.
  Deterioration of morale.
  Deterioration of personal appearance.
  Loss of interest in promotions.
  Apathy.
  Irritability.

- *Health/safety:*
  High accident rate.
  Carelessness evident.
  Needless risks taken.
  Safety of colleagues neglected.
  Loss of driver's license.

Source: Fair Oaks Hospital, (6).

---

company is making such a big deal over a few dollars. They can afford the loss," while an honest employee's typical response is, "They're getting what they deserve."

However, keep in mind that these are only trouble indicators. Not every person described by one of these indicators is dishonest, and each case must be carefully analyzed. Also note that some of these indicators point to the need for better employer/employee communication (see Chapter 6).

Why Do Employees Steal?

Why do employees steal? The obvious motive is to quickly obtain money or merchandise. Potential thieves in need of money believe that their situations make it impossible for them to get enough money by any honest means. Often, the need for money is due to:

- **Changes in financial responsibilities.** Recently married, widowed, or divorced employees often have new financial responsibilities. Other financial problems may occur when an employee's rent or mortgage payments increase, when employee's children begin attending special schools or colleges, or when a family member becomes ill or incapable of working for other reasons.

- **Living beyond means.** Sudden acquisition of elegant jewelry, expensive clothing, luxury cars, or other items may indicate that employees are living beyond their income. (However, employers must recognize that many employees come from dual-income households and may have the honest means to pay for such luxury items.)

- **Heavy drinking.** In addition to overt forms of theft, employees who are heavy drinkers may consume the facility's alcoholic beverages while at work and cause financial loss in terms of poor productivity or safety habits.

- **Gambling.** Compulsive gambling is a recognized cause of internal theft. In one study, 23 percent of 1000 respondents said gambling led them to embezzle company funds.

- **Serious debts.** Employees who are pressed by creditors find it tempting to dip into restaurant profits to pay their debts.

- **Using drugs.** Drug users need plenty of cash to support their habits.

Naturally, not all employees who need or want additional money become thieves. According to one security expert, "These types of needs should be considered *red flags*. They do not mean that an employee is involved in theft or that a loss will occur. They do mean that if the opportunity is also present and the employee's attitude is poor, the odds dramatically increase that the employee could become involved in theft." (8)

Other Motives for Theft

Not all employees steal solely for money or merchandise. According to a Justice Department study, "Employees who take from the company do not seem to be grossly impoverished, nor do they seem to be in precarious financial situations which might entice them to theft." (10) In fact, the study could not prove that employee theft was caused by economic pressures.

Rationalization

Rationalization is a key component of employee theft. Thieves often justify their acts by telling themselves that they are merely borrowing company money or property, and that they will pay back the company or return merchandise at a later date.

Beliefs

How an employee defines theft affects whether or not the person will become a thief. People learn to distinguish right from wrong during their formative years. According to a noted criminologist and sociologist, most people do not become completely honest or dishonest, but become "honest in some respects and in some circumstances, but dishonest in other respects and circumstances." (4)

Most employees would agree that taking money that is not rightfully theirs would be stealing, but in less clearcut cases, "Honesty and dishonesty are interpreted differently by many people. An act which may be dishonest to one person may, in good conscience, be an honest and acceptable act to another person." (7) For example, some employees would consider giving an unauthorized employee discount to a family member a form of theft, while others would find the practice acceptable. According to the Justice Department study, "The vast majority of employees do not see themselves as thieves or disloyal employees even though they may take company property occasionally." (10)

To avoid misunderstandings that result in theft, restaurateurs must define theft for employees by spelling out in writing exactly what is or is not acceptable behavior.

Job Dissatisfaction

Employees who are dissatisfied with their jobs are more likely to steal. (10) While many employers may have felt that the only manifestations of employee job dissatisfaction were high turnover and low productivity, a Justice Department study found that many employees who admitted stealing were not only dissatisfied with their jobs, but planned to leave them in the near future. (10) (It should be noted that low productivity is considered a form of theft because it affects a company's ability to earn profit.) According to the study, "Workers who had no long-term commitments to their employers, and those who felt dissatisfied or unjustly treated, were most likely to engage in production deviance and employee theft. Additionally, wages were found to be less important than job satisfaction and personal fulfillment in determining theft tendencies." (5)

The Justice Department study also found that worker dissatisfaction was particularly a problem for young and part-time workers. In many instances, these employees felt alienated from the company because they rarely received the benefits given to long-term employees. Theft rates for younger employees were lowest in companies that gave these employees the same benefits and privileges given to older or full-time workers. (10)

Peer Pressure on the Job

Some employees steal because they are influenced by dishonest co-workers. These employees may feel that everyone steals, so theft is necessary to be accepted by others. In other instances, employees protect dishonest co-workers by not reporting thefts to employers. Studies have shown that in many companies there are unwritten rules among employee groups that specify the type and amount of "acceptable" theft. Theft rates are highest in groups of employees that socialize during nonworking hours. (10)

Many restaurant operators discourage employees from forming overly close relationships by making periodic changes in employee and supervisor shifts and schedules and rotating job responsibilities. These actions can be effective theft deterrents if they are properly carried out and do not antagonize employees.

Perception of the Company and Its Managers

"Theft is in large part reflective of how management at all levels of the organization is perceived by the employee. This means that management can have an effect on the incidence of theft in the work organization." (10) Employees are more likely to steal from an organization when: (5, 8, 10)

- **The company lacks antitheft policies and procedures.** Companies that specify what is considered theft and how theft incidents will be handled suffer fewer losses.

- **Antitheft policies are poorly communicated.** "The first thing that virtually every employee who is caught stealing says is 'I can't believe I did this, why didn't someone tell me that I'd get in trouble.' Most employees assume that theft is management's responsibility, not theirs unless management tells them otherwise." (5)

- **Managers ignore shortages or employee theft incidents.** "[Managers'] response (or lack thereof) can be critical to the informal establishment of the tolerable limits of theft and deviance within the workplace on a day-to-day basis and the circumstances under which theft is permitted or not permitted. If supervisors tolerate various forms of deviance or react to its occurrence differentially, future acts of employee theft should be expected to reflect these past patterns of behavior and response." (10)

- **Companies do not carry out theft penalties when employees are caught.** If a company has a policy of prosecuting employees who steal, but only gives these employees warnings or, at the most, fires them, it may give other employees the impetus to steal.

- **There is a lack of fairness.** Employees are aware when discipline is not uniform or when some employees receive privileges not based on seniority or job responsibilities. Companies that stress integrity and fairness have fewer internal theft problems.

- **The company does not seem to care about employees.** This is indicated by sporadic or nonexistent salary and performance reviews. When managers are not interested in communicating with employees or in helping them develop professionally, the employees are less loyal to the organization. Furthermore, "Employees often related that their attitudes toward the company were most affected by the relationship with their immediate 'bosses' who were perceived to represent management at all levels. Thus, when work supervisors are not responsive to the needs of their employees, they can aggravate the deviance situation by providing a personal focus to the victimization." (10)

- **Managers set a poor example by giving unauthorized discounts to family and friends or by taking food and supplies.** The Justice Department found that manager behavior typically defines acceptable and nonacceptable behaviors. Managers who follow antitheft policies and procedures are good role models and experience fewer employee theft incidents in their facilities.

Opportunity

Dishonest employees steal when given the opportunity. Not surprisingly, restaurants that do not incorporate internal theft control as a component of their security policies and procedures have higher employee theft rates. But "most organizations, even those with tight controls, provide ample opportunity for theft." (3) Employees who are responsible for cash handling, accounting, purchasing, and inventory control have the greatest opportunities to steal. In order to fulfill their job functions, these employees have access to money or supplies. Typically, these employees also have fewer security restrictions than other employees (e.g., a receiver has unlimited access to the receiving area, from which most other employees are barred).

Limiting such opportunities to steal involves a system of checks and balances so no employee, regardless of job level, is left unaccountable. (Instituting such checks and balances is discussed in Chapter 4.)

Perceived Risk

The degree of perceived risk is a major factor in employee theft. According to the Justice Department, "The most consistent predictor of theft involvement was the employee's perceived chance of being caught. When the employee indicated that there was a significant possibility that 'I would be caught if I took something belonging to my employer,' less theft was likely to be found." (9)

Employees perceive that the risks of being caught are low when: (7)

- Companies have no antitheft policies or procedures.

- Employee theft policies and procedures are not communicated to employees on a regular basis.

- There is little concern about cash overages and shortages, or missing merchandise.

- Supplies are seldom inventoried.

- Cash registers are seldom audited.

- Professional shoppers are not used.

- Theft policies and procedures are enforced unevenly or not at all.

In other words, dishonest employees steal from restaurants when they have the need, have the opportunity, and perceive the risk is low.

3

Recognizing
Internal Theft

Types of Internal Theft

A cashier discovers a $5 bill beside the cash register drawer and remembers that the register was short that amount a few days earlier. Since no mention was made of the shortage, the cashier keeps the bill, assuming that the manager is either careless or does not consider the loss important. The next day, the cashier withholds another $5 bill, keeping it aside in case the shortage is questioned. Because no one says a word about the missing money, the cashier feels safe to continue the practice.

Employee thefts occur because of weaknesses in operating procedures, control systems, or supervision. When dishonest employees spot these weaknesses, they feel it may be safe to steal from the operation.

By identifying employee theft methods, operators can create or change control systems so there is less opportunity for future

29

incidents. *Solely identifying theft methods serves little purpose; the conditions which allow incidents to occur must be changed.*

There are many methods by which employees steal, but most are variations of embezzlement, pilferage, or misconduct. (Computer crime, an up-and-coming problem in restaurants, is discussed in the final chapter of this book.)

Embezzlement

Embezzlement refers to "the fraudulent appropriation of [money or] property by a person to whom it has been entrusted." (5) Examples of embezzlement include stealing from cash registers, falsifying accounting records, and accepting kickbacks. This type of theft occurs because employees are given more authority than necessary to fulfill their job responsibilities. (5)

Thefts of Cash Register Funds

The simplest form of embezzlement occurs when employees take money from cash registers or drawers. With the right controls, it is easily detected since the amount in the cash register or drawer will not agree with the register tape or guest-check totals. In other instances, employees responsible for taking payment:

- **Do not record the sale.** Those using cash registers may open the cash register by activating the cash drawer release latch or by ringing "No Sale." Others may leave the cash drawer open between transactions.

- **Fail to record the correct amount.** They charge the guest the correct amount, underring the sale, and take the difference between the amount rung up and the amount on the guest check.

- **Claim actual transactions as voids.** They record the correct total on the guest check, but then report the transaction as a void or overring and keep the money collected from the guest.

Warning signals of this type of theft include: (3)

- Transactions rung up incorrectly.
- Frequent overages or shortages.
- Open register drawers.
- Frequent void or "No Sale" rings.
- Paper and pencil, calculator, or adding machine placed next to register.

There are many variations of these theft methods. Among the most common are:

- **Bunching checks.** The practice of "bunching checks" or "lapping sales" is a variation of not ringing sales. When two or more identical checks are presented to the cashier, only one transaction is rung up on the cash register. Then a dishonest cashier can do one of two things, depending on the amount of cash received. If the exact amount is presented, the cashier simply pockets the money. If the cash is greater than the amount of the meal, the dishonest cashier puts the cash in the register, gives the guest change, and then pockets the amount of the meal when no one is looking. Since the check is not rung up, the cash register will balance at the end of the day.

- **Stiffing claims.** Dishonest servers or cashiers collect money from guests and give them the correct change, do not ring up the transaction, and falsely claim that the guests left the establishment without paying.

- **"Losing" checks.** This method is used in operations where servers present guests with numbered checks, collect money, and then give guests change. A dishonest employee will report a check as "lost." In actuality, the server has given the check to the guest, collected the money, given the guest change, and kept the money from the transaction.

- **Use of own checks.** Servers use their own guest checks instead of the facility's. None of these transactions are rung on the register. Instead, the server keeps all the funds collected from guests.

Cash Register Thefts Involving the Guest

In some cash register thefts, servers or cashiers steal from guests. However, in these cases the restaurant also loses. Guests become angry when they realize they've been cheated. The operation loses not only the guest's patronage, but sales from other guests because of bad word-of-mouth.

Cash register thefts where guests are victimized include:

- **Altering checks.** The server overcharges guests by charging them a higher price than the menu price or totaling their checks incorrectly. After guests pay the higher amount, the server adjusts the checks and keeps the difference. (Incorrectly adding so guests pay less in order to give friends discounts or to increase tips is discussed later.)

- **Giving guests incorrect change.** All transactions are rung up correctly, but the cashier or server gives the guests incorrect change. For example, if a guest pays for a $7.50 check with a $20 bill, the dishonest cashier or server gives the guest $2.50 change and keeps the additional $10. If the guest notices that the change is incorrect, the employee claims the guest paid with a $10 bill. While this is actually stealing from the guest, the restaurant also loses because many consumers are quick to spot "short changing" and may never again patronize the facility.

- **Switching checks.** Switching checks is prevalent in operations where servers collect the money from tables and take it to a cashier or to a cash register where they are responsible for making change. Suppose, for example, that a server has two parties—one with a $40 guest check and the other with a $50 check. A server presents the $50 check to the $40 table. If the party pays the $50, the server turns in only $40 and pockets $10. (If the party notices the "mistake," the server apologizes for the error and presents the correct check for $40.) Then the server presents the same $50 check to the second party, to whom it belongs. In a variation of this theft method, the server presents each party with the correct check, has the $40 sale rung up twice, and pockets the extra $10 from the $50 transaction.

Stealing from Co-workers

Some dishonest employees steal money from co-workers. For example, they may take a server's check, present it to a guest, collect and pocket the money, and return the check to the table. The second server then believes that the guest has left without paying. In other instances, dishonest employees may steal tips from tables or tip jars.

The Bar: A Special Problem Area

Bartenders can commit the same types of thefts as cashiers and servers. Bartenders can pour guests' drinks and not ring up the sales. Since the sales are never registered, the bartender feels relatively sure that the crime will go undetected. Or, the bartender can underring the price of a drink, charge the guest the correct price, and pocket the difference.

It is especially easy for bartenders to commit these crimes, because in some establishments, guests are not presented with guest checks.

Nor do they walk up to a register to pay for their drinks, so guests will not notice if the bartender is working out of an open register or hitting the "No Sale" key instead of ringing up the amount of the transaction.

- **Underpouring drinks.** Bartenders can underpour alcohol by as little as a quarter-ounce, and pocket the sale of the "extra" drinks.

- **Reporting drinks as spilled, returned, or complimentary.** In actuality, these are drinks that were sold but not rung up.

- **Reporting a bottle as missing or broken.** Bartenders can report a bottle as missing or broken and pocket the sales from the drinks made with the alcohol.

- **Bringing in alcohol.** By bringing in their own liquor, bartenders can keep all the income collected from the sales of drinks made with their alcohol.

- **Recording drink sales as bottle sales.** "Bartenders can accumulate drinks sold by the glass, record the accumulation as a bottle sale, and pocket the difference in cost." (1)

- **Diluting liquor.** Bartenders can dilute liquor and keep the income from other sales. In addition to hurting restaurant profits, diluting drinks results in less satisfied patrons and is illegal.

- **Using well brand instead of call brand and keeping the difference.** Bartenders can substitute well brands or less expensive brands when a guest orders a drink made with a premium liquor. The guest is charged a higher price for a premium drink, but a less expensive drink made with lower-quality alcohol is recorded. As with diluting drinks, this is a serious problem since substituting liquor without informing the guest is illegal in many states.

Embezzlement of Funds in Other Areas of the Facility

Types of embezzlement practiced by employees with inventory control or accounting responsibilities are usually more complicated and more damaging to restaurant profits. Thefts committed by accounting and inventory personnel are especially costly because these employees have opportunities for thefts that are not discovered until great damage has been done. Frequently used embezzlement techniques include:

- **Lapping funds.** Lapping refers to "the temporary withholding of receipts such as payments on accounts receivable. Lapping is a continuing scheme which usually starts with a small amount but can run into thousands of dollars before it is detected." (5) In lapping schemes, an employee responsible for recording payments may receive a payment from one guest, pocket the income received, and apply a portion of another guest's payment to the first guest's outstanding balance.

- **Payroll thefts.** Accounting employees may make out duplicate salary checks in their own names or they may make checks out to fictitious employees. They then watch for the original cancelled checks, take them out of the incoming mail from the bank, and destroy them. They try to conceal their actions and balance the accounts by raising the amount on several legitimate, cancelled checks. In other instances, employees may falsify overtime records or expense accounts or cash unclaimed wage checks.

- **Check-kiting.** Employees responsible for writing checks and making deposits to two or more bank accounts have the opportunity to "kite" checks. In a check-kiting scheme, the employee takes advantage of the period it takes for a deposited check to clear (this period is often called the "float"). An example of how a three-day float scheme works follows: (5)

  On the first day, a check for $1,000 is drawn on Bank 1 and deposited in Bank 2. The next day, the employee goes to Bank 2 and cashes a check for $1,000 drawn on the Bank 2 account. Before Bank 2 collects the money for the check drawn on Bank 1 (remember, in this example it takes three days), the employee deposits a check for $2,000 drawn on the Bank 2 account into the Bank 1 account. The check not only assures payment of the original kited check, it also increase the amount of the kite. This process is repeated, and the employee continues to collect money until one of the banks refuses to honor a kited check because the funds deposited are uncollected.

- **Stealing checks.** Employees may intercept a check payable to the company and forge the company's name; endorse the check to themselves; increase the face amount of a check or change the name of the payee; pay an invoice twice and appropriate the second check; or simply steal a check that has been made payable to cash.

- **Fictitious bookkeeping entries.** Purchasing employees with bookkeeping responsibilities can establish dummy suppliers. False purchasing orders and invoices are recorded, and checks made payable to the dummy suppliers are cashed by the purchasing employee.

- **Vendor kickbacks.** A buyer orders 250 pounds of large shrimp. The supplier delivers medium shrimp. Moreover, the delivery is 50 pounds short, a total of 200 rather than 250 pounds. The receiving clerk, who is in collusion with the buyer and the supplier, confirms that the order was filled according to the buyer's order. The restaurant pays a bill for 250 pounds of large shrimp. Then the receiving clerk and buyer receive a share of the profits from the vendor—a kickback. When employees work with suppliers to steal from a restaurant, it is a sad, costly situation. In some cases, only the buyer and a vendor representative are involved. In these instances, the buyer usually assumes the responsibility for inspecting incoming items. Forms of vendor collusion occur when:

  The buyer orders a certain quantity or quality of products, but has fewer and/or poorer quality products actually delivered to the restaurant.

  The buyer approves an inflated invoice and gets a kickback from the supplier on the overpayment. Invoices are inflated by making a deliberate error on prices or price extensions, or in totaling the bill.

  A delivery person delivers only a portion of an order to a restaurant, sells the balance to another restaurant, and splits the difference with a dishonest employee who signs for the first delivery that is never fully unloaded from the delivery truck.

  Buyers purchase second-grade products at first-grade prices and receive kickbacks. Because of normal variations in quality, such kickbacks are sometimes difficult to detect.

Theft of Merchandise or Supplies

Theft of merchandise or supplies is called pilferage when it refers to theft of company property by "employees who have access to merchandise but little or no access to company records or bookkeeping." (2)

Items That "Sneak Out"

One of the favorite employee theft routes is through the back door. Cartons of foodstuffs or supplies can be pushed near a rear door and tossed into an employee's car. The most common form of back door theft is to simply toss items out the door and have someone else come along later and pick them up. "The theft of raw food products out my back door is the worst single problem I encounter in my restaurants," said the operations vice president of one Florida-based chain. "There are so many variations of this that it is hard to keep up with them all."

When the back door is unavailable, there are many other routes open to employees. Steaks wrapped in aluminum foil can go out with the trash or laundry and be picked up later. Wine bottles concealed in overcoats are smuggled out. Meats and canned goods are dropped out of windows to be retrieved by friends. Food, candy, liquor, table linens, and dishes are hidden in handbags, briefcases, paper-wrapped packages, coat pockets, under coats, or elsewhere, and are taken home by employees. Silverware can be put in a pocket and carried out. Or, particularly in a fast-service operation, employees can hide items in their pockets, walk outside for a minute, and give them to friends in the parking lot.

Bar Area Thefts

The bar is a tempting target. Often bartenders operate without supervision. Sometimes there is a feeling that a little extra liquor will not be missed, that management does not care, or that employees are entitled to liquor as part of the rewards of their jobs. Sometimes bartenders give away free drinks to co-workers in exchange for high-cost food items like steaks. In still other cases, bartenders remove liquor from the premises either by pouring it into soft drink bottles, by taking the whole bottle and carrying it away with them, or by giving the bottle to an accomplice for removal.

Receiving and Storage Area Thefts

The receiving and storage areas are sources of tremendously expensive thefts—especially late at night or at other times when the restaurant is not as heavily supervised as during peak guest hours. Receiving personnel may steal items and report them as undelivered, damaged, or returned. Storage or issuing employees can commit similar thefts. Liquor bottles can be reported as broken and perishables can be reported as spoiled when these items have actually been stolen.

Thefts may also occur because storage areas are unsecured. In one case, a security specialist hired to investigate losses found that the night crew had worked together to steal inventory. The crew had found a weakness in the restaurant's security system. Every night a central alarm system preventing unauthorized entrances and exits was turned off for 15 minutes. The period was sufficient for the night crew to pass in and out several times, carrying armloads of merchandise.

Misconduct

Misconduct (also called counterproductive behavior or employee deviance) is an often overlooked form of theft. Examples of misconduct include "extended lunch and coffee breaks, work slowdowns, absenteeism, and inferior workmanship by employees. [As with forms of outright theft] these counterproductive behaviors also negatively affect the company, but are often not perceived as 'theft' due to their more innocuous nature and the greater difficulty involved in the assessment of their financial impact." (6)

Counterproductive behavior is a major problem that costs restaurants $120 billion each year. (4) Chart 3.1 shows what a daily loss of five minutes time per employee costs a restaurant annually.

Employee misconduct is not limited to poor productivity and other forms of "time theft." Misconduct also includes:

- **Unauthorized employee meals.** Employees often help themselves to the facility's food and beverages because they feel that free meals and drinks are a privilege of the job.

- **Giving complimentary or discounted meals.** Servers may give free or discounted meals to friends and relatives, or servers may

---

Chart 3.1. Yearly Cost of Five Minutes Lost Time Each Day Per Employee*

Hourly Wage	10 Workers	25 Workers	100 Workers
$3.35	$1,424	$3,559	$14,238
$4.50	1,913	4,781	19,125
$5.50	2,338	5,844	23,375
$6.50	2,763	6,906	27,625

* Based on 8-hour day, 5-day week, 255 working days per year.

Source: Nation's Restaurant News—Restaurant Technology. (4)

"forget" to transfer beverage sales to meal checks. Servers may do the same for guests with the hope that they will give them larger tips.

- **Giving stronger or complimentary drinks.** Bartenders may overpour drinks, either intentionally with the hope of receiving a larger tip, or accidentally because they are not using measuring utensils. Bartenders may also give some guests free drinks. Although some bartenders will insist that overpoured or complimentary drinks benefit the restaurant because the guest will feel special and patronize the restaurant more frequently, these practices are nonetheless costly.

As stressed in the beginning of this chapter, knowing employee theft methods is useful only when operators develop control systems to prevent future thefts. Theft-prevention techniques are of key importance.

4

Theft-control Techniques

Separation of Duties

Separation of inventory control, cash handling, and accounting responsibilities is the cornerstone of any theft control system. Theft opportunities exist because employees are given too much control in an operation or because they have greater access to funds or valuables than necessary to perform their job functions. When control of each of these areas is assigned to different employees, losses are minimized and inconsistencies or other problems are detected more quickly.

Inventory Control

All items must be tracked from the time they are ordered to their end use. This means that purchasing, receiving, storing and issuing, and production must all be monitored. Responsibilities for overseeing each function should be assigned to different employees to decrease theft opportunities.

Purchasing

Effective control begins with purchasing. The entire purchasing operation should be carefully supervised by managers above the food buyers' level to ensure the use of all appropriate controls.

Purchasing controls are necessary to prevent collusion between buyers and vendors. Purchasing controls include:

- **Competitive bidding.** Competitive bidding refers to the process of obtaining prices (bids) for predetermined quantities and qualities of products from a list of approved vendors, and buying from the vendor who submits the lowest bid. Buyers will not be able to accept payoffs from vendors in exchange for an order, nor will buyers be able to extort money from vendors.

- **Purchase orders and specifications are used.** These ensure that the correct quantities and qualities are ordered. (Purchase orders and specifications are discussed in the vendor theft section of Chapter 11.) Purchase orders can be compared to receiving documents, invoices, and bills, to ensure that the restaurant is only charged for items ordered and delivered.

Receiving

In most restaurants, receiving is not given the importance it deserves. Receiving responsibilities are often assigned to untrained personnel and there are often few, if any, checks on incoming merchandise. Dishonest employees may manipulate and falsify records in order to convert food into cash. In addition they may accept orders that are short on quantity, quality, or both. Therefore, it is especially important to check all items to be sure that the order matches the merchandise received. Receiving areas can be safeguarded from theft incidents by having good supervision, adequate physical protection, and sensible control systems and procedures. A little effort in establishing effective controls can go a long way to avoid the disastrous shortages that many restaurants suffer.

Only trustworthy employees should be given receiving responsibilities. Receivers should not have buying, storage control, or accounting responsibilities. Proper receiving controls include:

- **Keep the receiving area secure when not in use.** Doors should only be unlocked when scheduled deliveries arrive. Unauthorized personnel should never be permitted in the receiving area.

- **Check quantities and qualities.** Installing and using scales is one of the quickest and easiest ways to make certain that products are as ordered. Checking weights and quantities is especially important with portion-control meats. Liquor and nonfood items must also be checked upon delivery. When receiving liquor, it is important to check proof and bottle size in addition to the total number of bottles. Other specifications, such as brand name, must be checked as well.

- **Record delivery information on receiving documents and compare with purchase orders.** Products should be recorded on receiving forms. Receiving forms are compared to invoices and purchase orders to ensure that ordered products were received. Copies of receiving documents can be sent to bookkeeping and storage departments to ensure that the entire order is stored and paid for. This way, receivers will not be able to work in collusion with vendors. (By submitting receiving documents with invoices, managers and auditors can check the validity of paid invoices.)

- **Document deficiencies, returns, and damages.** Credit memos should be prepared in duplicate, so that they will not be ignored at the end of the month, and so that the accounting department can deduct the value of defective merchandise from the end-of-the-month statement. Any deficiency (short weights, other shortages, insufficient quality, back orders, errors in price, errors in extension, and deposit returns) should be recorded on these forms and initialed or signed by the receiver and the delivery person.

- **Examine invoices.** Invoices must be checked for errors in extensions and arithmetic. Prices must be those quoted. Most well-run establishments have audits performed to check invoices. Audits should be completed by managers, trusted employees, or in the case of larger establishments, an outside auditing firm.

Increasing numbers of restaurants are using another method to control receiving: making two or more people responsible for the task. In other establishments, owners, managers, assistant managers, or manager trainees perform receiving tasks.

Storing and Issuing

Naturally, all incoming shipments should be stored or refrigerated promptly. This prevents thefts and ensures that product quality is maintained. The system should provide a constant record of all goods on hand. Many operations accomplish this by recording products in a perpetual inventory record when they are stored. High-cost items are often recorded on stock cards, which are kept in an inventory book. Initial entries should indicate the date merchandise is received, along with its quantity and price. Entries are compared to receiving documents to ensure that there was no collusion between the delivery person and the receiver.

Merchandise should be made available to authorized kitchen employees only if they have a written requisition. Goods are recorded on the stock card when they are issued to kitchen personnel. Thus, the stock card can be used for periodic inventory reconciliation (opening inventory + purchases − recorded issues = expected closing inventory). By comparing inventory records with actual stock, management can tell if items have disappeared without a requisition and can follow up with an investigation.

Production Control

Control cannot be overlooked in the kitchen. In addition to deterring theft, production controls reduce spoilage losses and increase productivity. In addition to using requisition forms to get products from storage, many restaurants control production by using standardized recipes and portion-control products. Standardized recipes are used to produce menu items that are consistent in quality and quantity.

If standardized recipes are not used, production managers can consult quantity food production cookbooks and other sources to determine portion sizes. Examples of this form of portion control include:

- Using a three-quarter cup ladle to serve soups (first course portion).

- Serving 5- or 6-ounce portions of egg, tuna, or chicken salad.

- Cutting a double-layer sheet cake baked in 9-inch × 30-inch pans into thirty 3-inch × 3-inch portions.

Portion control products refer to menu items that are received by the facility ready-to-use and in predetermined amounts. Examples of portion control products include 4-ounce hamburger patties and 5-ounce breaded chicken cutlets.

By using these controls, managers can compare the quantity of prepared food in the kitchen with the quantity sold. The following equation is used:

$$QP - QS = QR$$

where:

QP = Quantity prepared (calculated using portion-control products or yield on standardized recipes).

QS = Quantity sold (calculated from guest check entries).

QR = Quantity prepared and remaining in the kitchen.

Any discrepancies should be discussed with appropriate employees to determine their causes.

Cash Register Controls

Cash register control begins with placing the cash register in a position that is highly visible to both guests and management. This makes it difficult for cashiers to throw out checks or ring identical checks only once. Also, it is wise to locate the cashier near the door so that guests have to walk directly past the register as they leave. This enables a supervisor stationed there to ask guests to pay their bills on the way out if the cashier does not do so. Following are some of the controls that are used.

Supervision

The manager, assistant manager, or supervisor should be designated to keep an eye on the cash register. Perhaps this responsibility can be divided among two or three persons but the signals should be clear as to who is watching at any given time.

Cashiers who know they are being watched will find it harder to steal, and the majority of cashiers who are honest will not mind the extra attention. Watching cash register operations involves very little extra effort and makes cashiers more efficient and careful.

A dining room manager, floor manager, or shift supervisor should be completely trained to enforce cash register rules. They should watch for unrecorded sales and open cash drawers, and should ensure that any cash register not in use is locked and that handbags and personal belongings are kept away from the registers. In addition, they should make certain that all overrings, voids, no sales, and credits are approved and that coupons have been properly used. Their vigilance is crucial, particularly in multiple-line systems.

It is also helpful when managers can recognize friends and relatives of employees and acknowledge them whenever they come into the restaurant. This lets the cashiers know that the supervisors recognize the visitors and may possibly be looking extra carefully when the visitors pay their bills at the register. In many operations, managers or supervisors will assume responsibility for accepting payment from employees' friends and relatives.

Management should always be sure that cashiers start off each day with a different bank of cash. Cashiers should never be allowed to keep their bank of money from the previous day. Instead, management should secure the money under their control.

Most emphatically, managers must notify each cashier of any violation of restaurant policy or of any daily shortages or overages. By discussing overages and shortages with cashiers, discrepancies do not get too far out of hand, cashiers are aware that errors will be detected immediately, and they understand that it will be difficult to get away with dishonest activity.

Rules and Regulations

Management should establish rules that are definite yet easily understood before assigning anyone to a cash register. When cashiers are hired, they should be given a written copy of the rules and asked to sign one copy, indicating that they have read and understand the rules and agree to abide by them.

How strict should rules be? It is up to management to find a balance between the effects of controls on service to guests, productivity, and employee morale, as well as the amount of loss that can be recovered through various types of controls.

The following are some rules which can be adapted to fit a restaurant's cash handling situation as well as management's operating philosophy:

- **When cashiers total a series of items (such as in a fast-service restaurant or cafeteria), they should call out the prices as they ring them.** This reassures guests that there is no overcharge and makes unauthorized discounting difficult.

- **The release lever must not be used to open the cash register drawer.** The release for opening the drawer should be kept locked at all times. Only the manager should have the key. If a guest asks for change, a "No Sale" or "No Change" should be rung to open the drawer.

- **Detail tapes should be replaced immediately when they run out.** Without a detail tape, the restaurant has no printed record of the transactions to uncover theft manipulations. Detail tapes should be checked at the start of each day and replaced if the supply gets low. Tapes should be checked to be sure they are in sequence.

- **Cash registers should be kept locked when not in use.** An unlocked, unattended register is an open invitation to steal. In-use registers should never be unattended.

- **Voids and overrings should be approved by the manager or supervisor.** This reduces the opportunity for cashiers to falsely claim actual transactions as errors.

Using Numbered Checks

One way to stop the practice of bunching checks or of giving free meals is to have all checks numbered consecutively. That way, if any checks are missing or lost, the problem will be noticed immediately and will be investigated. If every check must be accounted for, employees will be unable to throw out a check and pocket the money.

Numbered checks or blocks of checks should be issued to service personnel, who sign for them on a server's signature sheet. At the end of the day, each server's guest checks can be reconciled with a consecutive number record like the one in Chart 4.1. In this way management can detect any missing checks and trace them to the appropriate service personnel.

Accountability

Accountability is the essential ingredient of cash register controls. To employees, this means being answerable to occurrences within their area of responsibility. To management, it means being able to locate the source of a problem when checking on any transaction. State laws and restaurant policies vary as far as holding servers responsible for guest payment. However, accountability goes a long way in decreasing theft and increasing employees' alertness and sense of responsibility.

Accountability becomes even more important in the newer, more complex multiple-line cash registers and computerized terminal systems of modern fast-service operations. In these systems, several cash-

Chart 4.1. Guest Check Reconciliation Sheet

CONSECUTIVE NUMBER RECORD

HUNDRED_____   SERIES_____

WM. ALLEN & CO. STOCK FORM 7029

00	50	00	50	00	50	00	50	00	50
00	50	00	50	00	50	00	50	00	50
1	51	1	51	1	51	1	51	1	51
2	52	2	52	2	52	2	52	2	52
3	53	3	53	3	53	3	53	3	53
4	54	4	54	4	54	4	54	4	54
5	55	5	55	5	55	5	55	5	55
6	56	6	56	6	56	6	56	6	56
7	57	7	57	7	57	7	57	7	57
8	58	8	58	8	58	8	58	8	58
9	59	9	59	9	59	9	59	9	59
10	60	10	60	10	60	10	60	10	60
11	61	11	61	11	61	11	61	11	61
12	62	12	62	12	62	12	62	12	62
13	63	13	63	13	63	13	63	13	63
14	64	14	64	14	64	14	64	14	64
15	65	15	65	15	65	15	65	15	65
16	66	16	66	16	66	16	66	16	66
17	67	17	67	17	67	17	67	17	67
18	68	18	68	18	68	18	68	18	68
19	69	19	69	19	69	19	69	19	69
20	70	20	70	20	70	20	70	20	70
21	71	21	71	21	71	21	71	21	71
22	72	22	72	22	72	22	72	22	72
23	73	23	73	23	73	23	73	23	73
24	74	24	74	24	74	24	74	24	74
25	75	25	75	25	75	25	75	25	75
26	76	26	76	26	76	26	76	26	76
27	77	27	77	27	77	27	77	27	77
28	78	28	78	28	78	28	78	28	78
29	79	29	79	29	79	29	79	29	79
30	80	30	80	30	80	30	80	30	80
31	81	31	81	31	81	31	81	31	81
32	82	32	82	32	82	32	82	32	82
33	83	33	83	33	83	33	83	33	83
34	84	34	84	34	84	34	84	34	84
35	85	35	85	35	85	35	85	35	85
36	86	36	86	36	86	36	86	36	86
37	87	37	87	37	87	37	87	37	87
38	88	38	88	38	88	38	88	38	88
39	89	39	89	39	89	39	89	39	89
40	90	40	90	40	90	40	90	40	90
41	91	41	91	41	91	41	91	41	91
42	92	42	92	42	92	42	92	42	92
43	93	43	93	43	93	43	93	43	93
44	94	44	94	44	94	44	94	44	94
45	95	45	95	45	95	45	95	45	95
46	96	46	96	46	96	46	96	46	96
47	97	47	97	47	97	47	97	47	97
48	98	48	98	48	98	48	98	48	98
49	99	49	99	49	99	49	99	49	99

iers can be on duty at any time. All too often, a fast-service operation does not keep track of which cashier operates which register.

Whether registers are computerized or manual, there must be a system of strict accountability for each register or terminal drawer. To establish accountability, each cashier should have a separate cash drawer. If more than one cashier works from one drawer at the same time, there is no way to assign responsibility or determine blame when there is a shortage. If cashiers use the same drawer in sequence, they must sign in and out.

Some restaurants require cashiers to count and sign for the cash they receive at the start of their shifts. When they finish, they again count the cash and turn in a tally sheet showing the total. In other restaurants, cashiers merely deposit the cash in the drawer, to be counted by another person. In any case, it is a good idea not to give cashiers access to the total sales figure when the supervisor or manager takes the reading. Neither should they be given any idea how much money they should take in during their shifts. Such information gives cashiers an indication of how much money they could take and how to adjust their figures to avoid being caught.

As an added precaution, all cashiers should have their own keys and their own identifying numbers on the guest checks they ring. The guest checks should be compared with the cash receipts on the machine tape and with the final cash count. After the cashiers end their shifts, the supervisors should remove their cash drawers and make sure all the cash is counted. Although this is time-consuming, it is well worth the effort.

Auditing Techniques

Some operations do not provide cash receipts for guests unless they are asked by the guest to do so. Not having to provide receipts makes theft even more tempting to cashiers. This is another of the reasons why a careful auditing procedure is such an important security measure. Itemized detail tapes can be one of the most effective theft control devices because they produce clues to theft. Auditing cash register operations involves examining and reviewing records of all transactions. They should be thoroughly checked.

The following are key points to look for in examining register detail tapes:

- **Continuity of transaction numbers.** A break in the continuity of transaction numbers indicates a problem. If a register is closed out and reopened the same day with a fresh tape and a fresh bank of cash, a cashier can ring up all transactions, pocket the money, and destroy the detail tape. This procedure could pass detection unless the manager checks the continuity of detail tapes on succeeding days.

- **Overages or shortages.** A series of small overages could actually be more dangerous than an occasional shortage. Errors could cause shortages and may simply indicate that the person is not properly trained or is not accurate. But it is important to remember that an excess of overages or shortages often indicates theft.

- **Blank spots.** Blank spots, where no figures appear on a tape, may be caused by a skipping of the cash register machinery or they may be signs of tampering. These should be examined to determine their cause.

Surprise Audits

Surprise cash register audits can sometimes uncover theft immediately. If managers suspect that a certain cashier is stealing, they should have the supervisor take over the cashier's register suddenly during a lull. The supervisor should close the register momentarily, remove the cash tray and register detail tape, and replace the detail tape and cash tray with a new bank. The cashier can resume handling guests immediately. If there are two or more registers, those under scrutiny can be shut down until the audit is completed.

A supervisor should take the detail tape and cash drawer to the office for balancing. If major overages or shortages appear, an immediate investigation should be launched to determine whether the cashier is merely making errors or is stealing from the restaurant.

Summary of Precautions

The following are the primary requirements for security at the cash register:

- Locate the cash register in a strategic position near the exit.
- Assign a specific person to supervise the cash register operation and to monitor it.
- Establish a set of control rules for cashiers and stick to these rules.
- Establish accountability for each cashier at each register.
- Have a system of numbered checks whenever possible and account for them in consecutively numbered sequence.
- Use the detail tapes to look for clues of possible dishonesty.
- Periodically conduct surprise audits on all cash registers.

No matter how many registers there are, management must always keep in mind the vulnerability of this area. A cash register is always a tempting target for someone with dishonest motives. Although most cashiers are honest, management cannot afford to take chances. When cashiers steal, it is usually because it seems so easy. Management's task is to convince cashiers that theft will not be tolerated and disciplinary action will be taken.

Bar and Beverage Control

Cash Register Controls

As with other employees who use the cash register, bartenders should not have access to the cash register reading. If bartenders have no way of finding out what the day's sales amount to, it will be much more difficult for them to practice this type of theft.

Inventory Controls

Liquor goes through a number of points, from receiving to storing and issuing, before it gets to the bar. Internal thefts may occur at any one of these points; precautions should be taken at each checkpoint.

Liquor Receiving

Effective precautions in liquor receiving include:

- Counting the number of cases and comparing the count with the quantity shown on the invoices.

- Making sure that the brands and sizes of the bottles delivered are correct.

- Spot-checking the contents of every fifth case to be sure that every bottle is full and none is broken.

- Keeping an accurate record of shipments received to assure that the perpetual stock record is up-to-date.

Liquor Storage

Before it is issued to the bar, liquor should be kept in a locked storage area. Only one key to this room should be in circulation. If two or more people are authorized to issue liquor from the storeroom to the bar, they should use the same key.

   If at all possible, the person in possession of the key should be the person responsible for the liquor; namely, the steward or a trusted employee other than the bartender. This ensures a system of checks and balances.

Issuing and Inventory Control

As previously mentioned, liquor issuance to the bar should be made only upon the receipt of an authorized requisition, supported by the previous day's empty bottles. If empties cannot be replaced by the same kind of merchandise, either the par stock inventory should be adjusted or there should be a notation made on the liquor storeroom record explaining the missing bottles. The general manager should be advised of and should initial records of all such shortages.

A perpetual liquor storeroom inventory, based on the issuing records, should be maintained on a form like the one found in Chart 4.2. One form should be used for each brand and size of all bar merchandise stored. The underlying principle of this inventory control system is that by adding new shipments (number of bottles) and subtracting the bar issues, the "balance"—or stock on hand—can be determined at any time. This balance should be checked frequently against a physical count of the same brand and bottle size and should always be checked at the end of each month.

If there are fewer bottles in stock than there should be according to the inventory record, the shortage may be caused by accounting errors, pilferage, unrecorded par or other issues, breakage, employee consumption, or goods invoiced but not received. It is imperative that all causes be investigated immediately and corrected as soon as possible.

Bottle Replacement Control

The most widely used method of protection against pilferage and other irregularities at the bar is the par stock / bottle replacement / sales value control. This requires that a par stock listing be established at the bar. The par stock listing consists of the number of bottles of each brand required during the business peak period, plus one bottle as a safety margin. The listing of brands and numbers is posted at the bar and is also printed on the bar inventory and requisition form (see Chart 4.3).

Along with this, a routine is established whereby the empty bottles of all bar merchandise are accumulated throughout the day. Empty bottles are stored in a box; none are destroyed. At the end of each business day, the night bartender fills out the bar inventory and requisition form. This record is used to give the bartender the authority to replace the depleted merchandise the following day.

A person other than the bartender fills the liquor order and returns it with a duplicate copy of the requisition to the bar. The bartender

Chart 4.2. Sample Liquor Storeroom Inventory Sheet

William Allen & Co., N.Y., Stock Form 6198

MAX. _____
MIN. _____

FROM _____ TO _____

STORE ROOM PERPETUAL INVENTORY

19 ____

COMMODITY: _____
CLASSIFICATION NO. _____
PRICE PER UNIT: $ _____

UNIT: _____ LBS.

Month Date	REC'D	ISSUED	BAL.	REC'D	ISSUED	BAL.	REC'D	ISSUED	BAL.	REC'D	ISSUED	BAL.	REMARKS
on Hand													
1													
2													
3													
4													
5													
6													
7													
8													
9													
10													
11													
12													
13													
14													
15													
16													
17													
18													
19													
20													
21													
22													
23													
24													
25													
26													
27													
28													
29													
30													
31													
Totals													
on Hand													

Chart 4.3. Sample Bar Inventory and Requisition Form

WILLIAM ALLEN & CO., N. Y. STOCK FORM 7040

No. 24969

BAR INVENTORY AND REQUISITION

BAR No._____   DATE_____

LIST NO.	SIZE	DESCRIPTION	PAR STOCK	ON HAND	REQUISITION					INVENTORY	
					QUANT.	UNIT COST	TOTAL COST	UNIT SALE VALUE	TOTAL SALE VALUE	UNIT COST	TOTAL COST

INVENTORY TAKEN BY: ISSUED BY: RECEIVED BY:

on duty checks in the merchandise and signs the requisition/issuing record, verifying that the bottles recorded have been received.

This record then becomes the basis from which to calculate the previous day's bar cost and income. The calculation is made by multiplying the number of bottles issued (based on the returned empties of the previous day) times their cost and sales value.

The sales value of each bottle of liquor is determined by multiplying the number of drinks which can be served from each bottle (based on the ounce size per serving) times the selling price per drink. The product of sales value times replacement merchandise is recorded for enough days to allow for merchandise turnover—this record is then used as a base to estimate expected bar income. The resulting figure is compared to the actual cash received. If there are continuing bar shortages, they are discussed with bar personnel to make sure that the sales value calculations were correct and to make personnel aware of bar control procedures.

Security Measures at the Bar

In addition to using a par stock system, effective control of the bar includes using the following procedures:

- **Bartenders should use standardized recipes and measuring utensils to prepare drinks to avoid overpouring.**

- **A complete package inspection at the employees' entrance helps prevent personal bottles from being brought in from the outside.** In addition, managers should arrange to have bottles marked, either by placing a decal on each bottle or by coding the bottle with an indelible mark visible only under ultraviolet light. Such markings make it easy to detect bottles that come from the outside, since all old bottles must be turned in for new ones.

- **To remedy a bartenders' failure to ring up a sale, insist that all guests be given a cash register receipt for each drink ordered at the bar.** For table service, drinks should be entered on the guest check.

- **All complimentary drinks should be approved by the owner or manager.** These drinks can be recorded either on a guest check or on a cash register receipt, giving the reasons for the gratis drink. This way drink gifts can be controlled.

- **Prohibit on-premises drinking of alcoholic beverages by employees.** Drinking on the job is destructive and expensive. Without a formal prohibition, bartenders may feel free to drink or provide drinks to other employees.

- **State alcoholic beverage commissions periodically inspect bottles to check proof.** If they find bottles that are under proof, it is grounds for a liquor license suspension. For this reason, it is wise to engage shoppers to check alcoholic contents as well as compliance with serving and cash-handling procedures. The knowledge that there will be checks acts as a deterrent to bartenders who contemplate wrongdoing.

Automatic Liquor Dispensing Systems

Mechanized and electronic bar control systems are finding increasing acceptance among restaurateurs. Although conventional bar control systems alert management to irregularities that have already occurred, they do not always indicate how or where, and detection is sometimes difficult.

Automatic dispensing systems have the advantage that they prevent many of the irregularities which can occur. Preprogrammed liquor control registers automatically record the price of each drink at the same time that the drink is electronically dispensed. This avoids such irregularities as unrecorded sales, overpouring, or underpouring. It also reduces the possibility of human error.

Some of these devices are designed to dispense only predetermined quantities of liquor. Other more complex systems, which record the price as well, do not release the merchandise until the bartender pushes the proper button at the control register. This assures that every sale is priced and recorded accurately and is properly dispensed.

Among the advantages of electronic systems are:

- Uniform quantities of liquor dispensed.

- Prevention of overpouring and spillage.

- Positive inventory control.

- Elimination of pricing errors.

- Elimination of unrung sales.

- Improved productivity and speed in well-designed systems.

Restaurateurs should keep alert to advances made in these systems, and evaluate whether they would be useful in their operations.

5

Operating and Accounting Controls

Operating Controls

Restaurants require modern, professional theft control applications. Strong controls prevent theft in a number of ways. Not only do they reveal the extent of employee thefts, but they are often effective in identifying the thieves. Controls also let employees know what the facility considers desirable behavior on the job.

Entrance and Exit Control

For maximum theft control, one door—and one door only—should be designated as the authorized employee entrance and exit. This door should be used by all employees on all shifts. It might be the same door that guests use, but it should never be a receiving area door.

All unauthorized exit doors should be checked periodically to ensure that employees are not using them to remove stolen items. Restaurateurs might consider installing alarm systems on unauthorized doors as a precaution.

Key Control

Managers should guard against theft or duplication of any and all keys. Careless handling of keys makes it easy for anyone to enter a premises illegally. Keys should be given only to those employees who must have them to perform specific functions. Those employees should turn in their keys at a special control key box next to the employee exit when they leave each night. This helps monitor the key count and reduce the possibility that dishonest employees will make duplicates. If an early-morning employee or a late-night employee needs a key to open or close the facility, it may be necessary to make an exception to this rule. However, only under absolutely unavoidable circumstances should a key be taken from the premises.

A strong key control system should be a major part of every restaurant's security system, since a restaurant's insurance policy may not cover thefts resulting from negligence such as the loss of a key. (Guidelines for controlling keys and securing the premises with locks and alarms are discussed in Chapter 9.)

Package Controls

Some operations do not allow employees to bring any packages into or out of the restaurant, while others permit the practice as long as employees follow company policies and procedures. Because packages are convenient hiding places for stolen money or merchandise, restaurants need package controls. Facilities control packages by either conducting package inspections at the employee exit or by having a checkroom or other central area near the employee door where all personnel must check their property.

If package inspections are conducted, security personnel can randomly select a few individuals to check on each shift. Personnel should not be antagonized by overly long delays at the exit, nor be searched every time they enter or exit the facility.

When a checking system is used, restaurant operators need to familiarize themselves with their legal liability and insurance coverage for their employees' stored property.

Locker Room Security

In many restaurants, employees change into their uniforms and store their clothing in locker rooms. A locker room is a theft hazard, a place where employees can hide items or where they can exchange stolen items with each other.

Locker rooms should have very bright lighting at all times. Dimly lit areas help thieves steal. Lighting panels should be secured so lights cannot be switched off without a key or code.

Employees should not be allowed to carry personal belongings from the locker room into the storage area or any other place where there is food or money.

Specific locker room procedures should be posted, all lockers should be kept locked, and personnel should be assigned to monitor the area.

Trash Removal Control

Thieves hide stolen items in trash cans or bags, remove them to trash storage areas, and retrieve the items when it is convenient. Therefore, a supervisor or security person should be present when trash is loaded onto a truck, and outgoing trash should be spot-checked for hidden items.

If trash is burned in an on-premises incinerator, the refuse area or incinerator room must be periodically checked. Such checks are a deterrent to employees who might use their trash-burning duties for dishonest purposes.

Closed-Circuit Television

Many experts in the security field believe there is more to be lost than gained by installing closed-circuit television to catch dishonest employees. The amount of antagonism aroused by such a system sometimes incites employees to challenge the television cameras rather than be deterred by them. However, many restaurant operators, particularly those in large facilities, believe closed-circuit television is a useful theft deterrent in receiving areas, cash rooms, and other areas containing valuables.

Integrity Shoppers

Some restaurants employ anonymous "shoppers," on either a full-time or part-time basis, to eat in their units and file reports on such matters as the quality of the food; the caliber, speed, and courtesy of service; and the overall atmosphere and cleanliness of the facility. They usually give performance ratings to servers and cashiers.

Because of the severe internal theft problems that some companies encounter, their shoppers also test the honesty of facility personnel. They test up-front control systems by assessing how their payments are handled. They also use techniques, such as deliberately handing a cashier an overpayment, to see what occurs.

Controls at Closing Time

Perhaps the most critical period in theft control occurs when the restaurant is closed for the night. Management should make certain that all storage rooms or closets are locked, nobody is hiding in the rest rooms or lockers, the night lights are on, food and beverages have been stored and secured, windows and doors are locked, and any alarm systems are activated.

A quick inspection of the entire building should reveal whether an employee is hiding in some inconspicuous area. A checklist can be used to ensure that no area is overlooked. (Additional closing precautions are discussed in Chapter 9.)

Internal Accounting Controls

A good internal control system has cross-checks for every major control procedure. As a rule, the person who does the ordering should not be the same person who approves invoice payments. The degree of separation of responsibilities depends on the size of the restaurant operation. In a small company, the manager or owner may become a part-time internal auditor—checking transactions, confirming items, and investigating original documents. Regardless of restaurant size, the restaurant accounting control program should include the following tasks to be performed or monitored by owner/managers:

- Deposit all cash receipts intact daily.

- Make all payments by bank check and countersign them.

- Reconcile bank account statements each month.

- Spot-check bank balances during different periods each month.

- Check guest statements against house accounts receivable before mailing statements.

- Open all incoming mail promptly.

- Compare cash receipts with books and with deposits shown on bank statements.

- Do not let bookkeepers handle receiving tasks.

- Bond bookkeepers for a suitable amount of money.

- Log incoming checks. Compare this list with the cash receipts ledger.

- Record interest payments, rents, and other miscellaneous income so that any failure to get a receipt can be investigated if necessary.

- Process credit card receipts promptly.

- Have the duties of a cashier, accounts receivable bookkeeper, and general bookkeeper performed by different people.

- Have the general bookkeeper maintain a record of negotiable notes and securities, and secure the actual documents so comparisons can be made.

- Require documentation such as purpose of expense and receipts for petty cash disbursements.

- Control check distribution:
  Use serially numbered safety paper for checks.
  Use permanent ink or check-writing machines.
  Never sign blank checks.
  Enter amounts legibly.
  Write check number and payment date in ink on supporting documents.

- Pay all employees by check.

- Audit pay rates occasionally to make sure the proper amounts are being paid to each employee.

- Have people other than those who keep the cash records reconcile monthly bank statements and cancelled checks with the general books.

- Examine cancelled checks, signatures, and endorsements, and return the checks to the bank when necessary.

- Be sure that all credits to accounts other than those arising from cash remittances and cash discounts receive approval from an authority other than the cashier or accounts receivable bookkeeper.

- Ensure that only a responsible executive has the authority to write off bad debts.

- Keep complete control over records of bad debts that are less than three years old.

- Mail guests who have house accounts a special statement at least once a year to be sure they agree with the accounts receivable records. Such a mailing should be initiated by an auditor.

- Be sure that accounting methods, routines, and control systems are detailed in written instructions.

- Change the safe combination periodically.

Outside Audits

Outside audits help restaurateurs keep their employees honest, but they do not replace the need for the manager to monitor the operation. Following are suggestions to make audits more beneficial to a restaurant operator:

- **Have as much line involvement as possible.** Let supervisors help decide which areas of performance are to be audited and how the information gathered is to be used.

- **Use horizontal rather than vertical reporting.** Gathered information should be made available directly to the person who needs it to help solve a problem. The information should be available to higher levels only if the problem is not corrected. In this manner, members of the staff will be less likely to hide or falsify information. They will also be less likely to feel threatened.

- **Reward auditors or consultants for helping find constructive means to solve problems as well as for identifying problem areas.**

- **Initiate useful feedback.** The faster the auditing information is fed back, the more useful it is to the organization.

Discovering How Theft Can Occur

Unfortunately, even using the controls discussed, thefts may occur. Many managers dismiss employees caught stealing without ever trying to determine why the theft problem occurred. Too often, theft situations are seen as individual incidents. Instead, managers should consider these incidents to be symptoms of problems that may exist in the operation. It is important to discover the causes of these problems.

In situations with repeated theft incidents, each case must be analyzed to uncover the underlying causes of the situation and develop effective countermeasures to prevent such thefts from recurring. An intensive review can reveal physical limitations, weaknesses in control systems, and unsatisfactory supervision. A review can also indicate specific weaknesses, such as the lack of physical barriers or the presence of inadequate locks. It can reveal which controls are ineffective or missing entirely, and which management practices and employee attitudes need to be changed. Ironically, the greatest value achieved from apprehending a dishonest employee may not be removing a thief from the restaurant operation. It may be the stimulus to tighten the restaurant's security measures and increase enforcement of policies and procedures.

Managers can also use exit interviews to determine theft methods. These are useful in questioning employees about the types of theft they observed in the facility.

Usually, there are several possible causes for any given theft situation. By analyzing the situation step-by-step, the possible causes can be reduced to a limited number. This isolated group of causes can be examined and tested with relatively little effort.

How can the review be undertaken without apprehending a suspect in a theft situation? If it is known that heavy shortages exist but that a suspect has not yet been identified, each element in the control procedures system must be carefully checked. Next, the adequacy of enforcement procedures should be scrutinized. Then, the physical layout at the back of the restaurant, the front, and the cash register positions must be examined.

It is always easier to analyze the situation when there is a suspect. This at least provides a starting point for probing the real causes of the restaurant's losses.

Committee Review

Restaurants should have a program requiring the systematic review of any internal theft incident within a reasonable period after the employee is caught. A practical systematic program can be organized using the following suggestions:

- **Launch a program to gain maximum insight into every theft case by organizing a case analysis committee.** Its role should be to analyze every case, spot the causes of the theft, and identify the operating weaknesses which allowed the theft to occur.

- **Set a specific day and time for a committee review of any theft cases that have occurred.** Give the committee the facts in the case beforehand so they are prepared to discuss causes and possible countermeasures.

- **Start the meeting by reading a summary of the case to refresh the minds of the members and to provide any further details.** Be sure that all committee members have the facts relating to the incident. Encourage them to ask questions to be sure they understand the case. They should be familiar with these specifics:

  The method of theft.

  Length of time covered by the thefts and their frequency.

  Amount of money stolen and/or value and description of property stolen.

  Extent of admitted thefts.

  Whether or not there were accomplices.

  Any other details; e.g., what might have triggered the thefts, or the number of people involved.

- **The committee can then discuss how such thefts could be prevented.** In essence, it should determine who the dishonest employees are, how they were screened prior to hiring, and if there were any negative factors which should have made the restaurant more cautious. It should also consider evaluations by supervisors and whether suspicions had been reported to anyone.

- **If the committee has explored the entire problem in a logical fashion, it should reach some important decisions for improving restaurant operations, supervision, security, or control systems and procedures.** Once the committee decides what action to take, corrective measures should be assigned to appropriate personnel. If the problem is complex and requires a multi-sided approach, it may be advisable for the committee to establish an action timetable. In addition, intermediate reports should be made to determine progress toward correcting the nderlying causes of the theft problem. Then a follow-up should be made by a manager appointed by the committee to see that the plan or corrective action is being carried out as intended.

When properly analyzed, every internal theft incident can disclose important information to management—facts that can improve internal controls and supervision, managements' relationship with employees, and employee attitudes and morale. This can all be done quickly, efficiently, and with remarkable results by limiting the sources and causes of potential internal thefts.

6

Communicating with Employees

Policies and Procedures Are the Base

Security experts believe internal theft can be inhibited by having effective policies and procedures that let employees know theft will not be tolerated, and by visibly enforcing the rules.

Effective theft-deterrent policies and procedures specify employee conduct in regard to handling food, money, and other property and are communicated to employees:

- In job orientation sessions.

- By displaying the regulations in writing at locations where they are frequently seen.

- In training meetings and seminars.

- Through in-house publications.

Carefully constructed security policies and procedures convey to employees that theft has a destructive influence on a restaurant both financially and morally. Surprisingly, many employees are not aware that restaurants operate on low-profit margins that can be erased by theft incidents. Employees need to be aware that even taking small items, such as food snacks, is detrimental to the facility.

It is usually a facility manager's responsibility to make sure that employees receive security training. "The manager has the responsibility to see that the security system is not intended just to 'catch crooks,' but to help keep honest employees honest . . . Employees should neither resent nor fear the use of a security control system that protects them from any possible allegation of wrongdoing . . . Likewise, no system within the food and beverage operation can work without the cooperation of affected employees." (2)

Honest employees are not adversely affected by rules. When enforced properly and equitably, appropriate policies and procedures substantially reduce employee frustration and theft. People are actually more content when they are part of a well-disciplined, well-run operation. They respond favorably to the sense of emotional security on the job.

The Workplace's Emotional Climate

The emotional climate of the workplace is irrefutably linked to the amount of internal theft. A good working climate is a critical theft deterrent. Managers must recognize employees' need for emotional security on the job and keep in mind the following principles:

- The primary task of any restaurant supervisor is to motivate employees.

- Every employee needs emotional job security. This can be achieved by direct communication with the supervisor.

- When supervisors do not satisfy their employees' emotional needs through direct communication, they foster feelings of insecurity.

Proper human resources training helps supervisors recognize how to meet their employees' needs. Employees need reassurance in job performance, job standing, supervisory treatment, and job evaluation. Employees want to know:

- What is expected of them.

- Whether or not they are doing a "good" job.

- How their behavior and performance will be evaluated, and by whom.

- The results of their evaluations.

- The criteria managers use to determine promotions, raises, and bonuses.

People have a basic need for understanding and appreciation, and most people want to be rewarded for their efforts. Rewards can be monetary, or raising employees' self-esteem through praise for a job well done.

Employee morale is a significant force in maintaining an effective security program. Good morale decreases security problems remarkably. One of the most important ways of raising employee morale is to indicate an openness and willingness to listed to employees' ideas and problems. Even if little can be done to solve a problem, the concern and interest expressed by a manager may be supportive enough to sustain the employee.

Many employees would welcome a chance to discuss concerns with their supervisors, but few actually do because they do not feel free to express their opinions. Supervisors who invite employee discussions can make significant contributions to both the employees and the restaurant.

To help employees manage their feelings, supervisors need effective communication skills. The most effective way to aid employees is by helping them acquire more insight into their feelings and problems. This form of communicating helps employees discover solutions by themselves.

Effective Listening As A Tool

Managers who want to be effective in communicating with employees first need to develop the ability to listen. Listening to another person's account of feelings and problems requires concentration to grasp the attitudes and thoughts behind what is being expressed. Listening means showing genuine understanding and concern. If listeners indicate doubt, surprise, disagreement, or criticism, this at once places them in the undesirable role of judge or critic and impedes the communications process. (1)

Restaurant managers face numerous responsibilities and distractions. When an employee is speaking, they may feel that circumstances prevent their concentrating on much of what the employee is saying. Or, they may not be paying sufficient attention to interpret the employee's feelings accurately or objectively. Thus, they may arrive at false conclusions.

To avoid these dangers, managers must attend to what employees say and avoid doing other tasks when employees are trying to communicate. Writing a note or paying attention to other desk work indicates ignorance, bad manners, and a lack of concern. Employees receive the impression that managers are not listening and do not care. Even taking notes on conversations with employees can be distracting.

Prejudices also block communication. If managers do not like certain individuals, they will be less likely to be neutral and effective when listening to them. They must be as fair as possible to every employee, and not allow any preconceived notions about the employees and their honesty interfere with their ability to listen.

If a manager finds it impossible to conduct a productive conversation, arrangements should be made for the employee to speak with another supervisor who can be objective and deal with the employee in a helpful manner.

Nonverbal Communication

Nonverbal messages conveyed by facial expressions or gestures are sometimes more powerful than what is stated verbally. The supervisor's body language can act to encourage or discourage communicating. Looking warmly and directly at someone shows interest and concern. Leaning toward the person is also a sign of interest in what is being said.

When communicating, managers must appear relaxed. Establishing a warm, friendly, open atmosphere by thoughtful use of posture and expression is welcoming to an employee. It helps employees speak openly because it is indicative that the supervisor will respect any confidences.

Reflective Statements Provide Feedback

An important aspect of communicating is to provide feedback after listening to employees. Good communicators listen and accept employees' facts, arguments, reasons, explanations, stories of events, and justifications. After listening, a good communicator attempts to reflect the employee's feelings about the situation. When managers stay alert to how the employee feels, listen closely, and then summarize the employee's feelings, there is less chance of misunderstandings. Reflective listening also enables the employee to perceive the situation with insight.

For example, an employee tells a manager about a co-worker whom the employee describes as, "Lazy. Won't do the job. Unfair to everyone else who has to carry an extra share of the burden." At this point the manager might say, "You don't feel this person is assuming a fair share of the responsibility." This is a neutral statement that lets the employee know the manager is listening and understands.

The employee may now continue with, "That's right. I'm tired of covering because another person chooses to come in late all the time." Here is where the manager might summarize the feelings expressed with a reflective statement like, "So you feel that this person is shirking responsibilities." This is feedback of the employee's comment. The manager has remembered in reflecting the employee's comments to use different words from those of the employee and to make comments that are neutral in tone, not revealing any approval or disapproval.

Managers must remember when starting a communicating session with an employee to put the employee at ease. They might start with some discussion of sports of the weather, just to show that they are human and to put the employee at ease. If feasible, the manager should sit on the same side of the desk as the employee so that the desk does not become a barrier. No interruptions or distractions should be permitted during the interview. All incoming calls should be held. The employee must have the manager's complete attention.

The Right Questions

Questioning is another important part of communicating. In the beginning of a discussion, it is important not to ask too many questions. They tend to lead and direct the conversation. What is more, the employee could give the manager answers designed to please the manager, not to reveal the employee's feelings. Questions thwart open comments and expressions of feelings. Even worse, they can put an emotionally upset employee in a difficult position, since the employee might have no idea how to answer some of the questions.

Instead of asking questions about specific issues, the manager might ask general questions and be noncommittal. The object should be to draw the employee out, to encourage the expression of feelings, not just facts. For this purpose, the manager can effectively use neutral questions such as, "In what way did that bother you?" "How do you feel about that?" "Why do you think she didn't understand?" These are all leading questions that make conversation easier.

Questions which call for "yes" and "no" answers can defeat the purpose of getting the employee to talk. "Why" questions generally encourage greater thought and reflection.

It is best not to interrupt the employee. It is important to keep the employee's conversation moving. The right question can encourage the flow of facts and feelings, but the wrong question can interrupt or block the employee's thoughts.

Finally, questions regarding the outcome of an action can help an individual explore various solutions or consequences. Such questions as, "What do you think would happen if you did that?" "Do you think you could eventually adjust to that?" or "How do you think that would affect others?" encourage a person to explore the matter. This can often lead to the recognition of whether a solution is possible, whether it is effective, or whether it is merely a stopgap.

A good questioner leads an employee to discover the most practical and logical solution for a given situation. The best solution is an individual one, worked out in the context of an individual's own sense of values.

The best tactic for a manager to use if an employee asks for advice is to indicate that the best answer will be the one which the employee finds. Tactics that might be used to turn back the inquiry to the employee are, "How do you feel about that?" "What is your opinion about it?" "I think it would be best for you to tell me about it." "I'd be interested to learn just what you think can be done."

Even when a manager feels that an employee is off track, it is important not to challenge the employee's statements or to argue. This if often difficult, especially when the manager feels confident in seeing the problem more clearly than the employee does. However, it is most important to let the employee develop conclusions from the employee's own insights.

"Silence is golden" is an axiom which has a very real place at moments during conversations of a consulting nature. Silence at the appropriate time can be considerably more constructive than a whole series of questions and answers. If an employee is silent, the manager may think the person has stopped communicating. The employee may, instead, be thinking over the problem. If the manager can remain silent, the employee will usually initiate conversation again. The employee's silence is a healthy indication that the employee has taken time to review the situation. If the silence becomes uncomfortably long and it seems that the employee is finding it difficult to continue, it might be helpful for the manager to ask a question or make a statement that calls for further comment.

Other Considerations

Managers must always remember that if employees manifest hostile feelings toward them, more often than not the employees' comments result from their own personal fears or anxieties. These are rarely personal attacks. It may be that the employees feel inadequate in dealing with managers. Or, they may feel threatened by some of the manager's actions or comments. If this is the case, it is necessary for managers to understand why employees feel threatened by them.

Under no circumstances should conversations between managers and employees be allowed to deteriorate into unpleasant exchanges. If a manager has difficulty dealing with an employee, the conversation should be terminated and another solution sought.

It is wise to place a time limit on conversations with employees. One hour is usually sufficient. If this is made known when the meeting begins, the employee will know there is a full hour to discuss the problem. If the discussion seems to be running on without end, however, the manager will have a reason to terminate the meeting without trying to find an excuse or offending the employee.

If a second interview seems in order, the manager should let the employee suggest meeting again. If the manager wants to take the initiative, it should be done in a way that does not threaten or push the employee. "If you'd like to talk this over further, please feel free to stop by any time" is an encouraging, non-threatening way of giving the employee the choice. If the employee wants to meet again, the meeting should be scheduled at a time which allows the employee to think over and act upon the findings of the first meeting.

Some effective communications principles for managers include the following:

- Communicating with employees is part of a manager's job and may help prevent theft, waste, and abuse of company property.

- Managers guide employees toward reaching their own conclusions.

- By showing respect and concern for their problems, managers can help employees feel more comfortable and relaxed during communicating sessions.

- It is critical to be a good listener, concentrate on what is being said, and reflect an employee's feelings.

- Managers should ask neutral questions that will lead employees in a natural sequence from one point to another, without passing judgment on what employees say.

- Managers can help employees explore possible solutions by asking questions indicating possible consequences of the solutions.

- Employees need to be assured that what they say will be held in confidence.

Special Communication Skills Are Needed When Employees Have Drug and Alcohol Problems

Substance abuse has become such a problem in the workplace that many operations have instituted drug testing and/or employee rehabilitation programs. The warning signs of substance abuse were discussed in Chapter 2. Fair Oaks Hospital recommends that supervisors follow the guidelines listed below when they suspect an employee has a drug or alcohol problem: (3)

- **Document.** Have consistent documentation of the problem. Factual and accurate documentation of work-related deficiencies cannot be disputed.

- **Intervene.** Early intervention is important. Problems will not improve or disappear on their own.

- **Stick to the facts.** At the time of intervention, have the documentation in front of you. This will allow you to maintain control of the intervention. Don't rely on memory.

- **Remain objective.** Don't moralize or lecture. Do not become angry or allow the employee to discuss your own habits or personal life. Avoid meaningless threats of disciplinary action. If there is a threat, there must be a commitment to follow through. Getting subjectively involved may impair your ability to identify problems.

- **Have a treatment option available.** Know the agencies, treatment facilities, and consultants available to your employee. Make a referral to an appropriate source. If possible, aid your employee in making an appointment. Accent the confidentiality your company will grant the employee once treatment or help is sought.

- **Do not act as diagnostician.** Diagnosis should be left to those who are professionally trained.

7

Using Detectives to Investigate Theft

The Detective's Role

Occasionally, restaurateurs are faced with puzzling internal thefts. Although they have made every attempt to identify the source of the problem, they have been unable to stop the thefts or identify the methods or perpetrators. This is the point at which some restaurateurs (usually those in larger facilities) hire security investigators to detect the causes and find those responsible.

Detectives either are hired from outside agencies, or they are employees of the restaurant's own security system. Company policy usually specifies who has the authority to hire investigative personnel and how investigations should be handled. Because it is relatively expensive to hire experienced detectives, operators assess potential recoveries and possible further losses before proceeding to do so. (Irrespective of cost or recovery factors, some restaurateurs are opposed to using undercover detectives on philosophical grounds—they are opposed to

73

"spying" for any reason.)
   Restaurateurs hire detectives to:

- **Look for causes of unexplained cash or inventory shortages.** The causes of shortages are frequently difficult to pinpoint. When there is no obvious explanation, restaurateurs have the tendency to assume that thefts are the root of the problem. A detective can get close enough to the operation to find out whether the shortages are a result of theft, human error, or both.

- **Uncover after-hours thefts.** Employees who work very early or very late hours generally have a greater opportunity to steal than those who work regular hours. Because these employees are often poorly supervised, they may steal because they sense that there is little risk of being caught.

- **Expose theft rings.** In recent years, there has been a noticeable shift from thefts committed by individuals to those carried out by theft rings. Rings create a more serious threat to restaurant profits, because more is taken. Sometimes, the only way to combat theft rings is by using undercover detectives.

- **Discover the theft methods used by dishonest employees.** Discovering what loopholes in the company's security policies and procedures have contributed to the occurrence of crimes is as important as finding the perpetrators. Companies hire detectives to spot such problems and suggest remedies for them.

- **Find evidence for either apprehending or clearing suspected thieves.** Frequently, by using their intuition and monitoring the operation, restaurant operators come to suspect employees, vendors, or others of theft. Without evidence, it is difficult for restaurateurs to take action. In such situations, their tendency is to believe the worst, but often suspicions are unfounded. Detectives are hired to reveal the truth. Sometimes, these detectives go undercover as co-workers of suspects to be in a better position to confirm suspects' guilt or exonerate them.

Establishing an Undercover Program

When undercover detectives are needed, restaurateurs must be sure to hire only experienced, knowledgeable agents. A few very large food-service companies have personnel on their payroll who can work undercover in their restaurants.

When detectives are permanent employees, they develop company loyalty. The longer they work for the company, the more accepted they become by other employees. They are familiar with the company's philosophy and goals and thoroughly learn the company's control systems and procedures. Since they meet supervisors and employees throughout the company or facility, they have more insight than outsiders into problem situations. At the same time, top managers get to know their own agents and to understand them—what motivates them, how to evaluate their reports, and how to work with them to improve the overall operation. An agent who is a permanent employee can be transferred from one job to another when the need arises. Employees in other departments more readily accept an established employee than a newly hired one.

Despite the benefits of having in-house undercover detectives, there are drawbacks. They are costly, may become known to employees or too friendly with them, and may become so familiar with the operation that they are unable to have a fresh perspective on problems. Most restaurant operators are likely to hire undercover personnel from outside detective agencies.

When restaurateurs use a detective agency, they should assign a member of top management to work closely with the agency detective. The agency should provide the manager with a full report on the experience of the proposed undercover detective, which contains information on how long the agent has been with the agency, whether the agent has been screened for a police record, what type of training the agent has had, and what types of cases the agent has solved.

Restaurateurs specify the nature of the information they expect the detective to provide, as well as when and how they want it presented. They should make it clear that they do not want reports on extraneous matters or on minor rules infractions, and that they want to hear from the agent only when the agent has significant information. They should personally brief the agent on the facts of the situation and the objectives of the investigation, and they should ensure that the agent receives specific training in procedures related to the assignment.

Agent Selection

Restaurateurs must be careful when hiring an undercover agent. The wrong choice can be costly, since the agent could be either ineffective or dishonest, or both. It is imperative that the detective's background be thoroughly checked. There are special qualities beyond basic honesty that an undercover agent must have. Role-playing ability is especially helpful. Undercover agents must often say things contrary to their own beliefs in order to become accepted and gain the trust and confidence of co-workers.

If agents find they cannot play certain parts, they should be able to admit this. Not every person can be comfortable in every role.

Agents should have analytical ability. Since they constantly have to match wits with dishonest employees, it is essential that they have a sharp mind. They need to adapt quickly to emergencies and be able to see how bits and pieces of information interrelate.

Agents should be knowledgeable about the tasks they will be expected to perform in the cover jobs to which they are assigned. Moreover, if they are assigned to areas where most workers speak another language, they must know and speak that language—at the appropriate level—if they are to be effective.

Naturally, they need to be emotionally stable and self-controlled to deal with the pressures of undercover work. Finally, they must be patient.

Contract Provisions

Even extremely capable agents who have been hired on a long-term basis will have to be dismissed if their cover is "blown." To avoid arguments in such situations, agents should sign contracts specifying that they can be discharged without notice. It is wise to arrange two- or three-month automatically renewable contracts. Under no circumstances should managers be forced to keep an agent as a permanent employee if the agent's effectiveness has been destroyed.

Paying agents may require special arrangements. The agents should receive their pay for their cover jobs in exactly the same fashion as their co-workers. Additional pay can be given to the agent on a voucher, but it is preferable to pay it in cash. It is imperative that the agent's extra salary not be noted on the official payroll and that no one in the bookkeeping department know the agent's identity.

Protecting an Agent's Identity

Agents who have worked for other restaurants often require a new identity, in case anyone in the facility has ties with the other operations that could "blow" the agent's cover. The agent will require a fictitious name, background, and personnel records. The name selected should be similar to the agent's real name so the agent readily responds to it. Often the agent's real first name is used with a fictitious last name.

The agent's identity must be protected at all times. Under no circumstances should the agent's identity ever be revealed to the supervisor of the department to which the agent is assigned. Only the individuals who hired the agent should know the person's true function in the organization.

The only way to protect an agent's identity for the time required to build up the agent's effectiveness is for management to select well-trained professionals and to keep the situation confidential. If an agent is discovered or betrayed, the result can be worse than failure to complete the original assignment. It can sometimes lead to violence or a deterioration in the relationship between management and employees.

After an agent has left an assignment, managers may be tempted to relax and reveal the agent's mission in the company. This should be avoided. Employees do not enjoy knowing they were under surveillance. For this reason, an agent should not appear in court as a witness. Instead, management should arrange to have the agent provide evidence in such a manner that managers may present it in court.

To divert employee suspicion of an agent's true function, it is a good idea to have the agent brought in for questioning along with other suspects.

After agents have completed their missions, they should be moved to new areas. It is wise to keep using these specialists as troubleshooters in key areas so that the restaurant can gain maximum return for the agents' efforts.

Reporting Schedule

Even the most astute undercover agent should not be expected to provide instant revelations. It takes time to gain the confidence of co-workers. It is counterproductive for employers to pressure an agent for daily or weekly reports when there is nothing to report. This procedure could result in fabricated or inflated reports. The employer and the agent should have the mutual understanding that the agent will report only when there is something worthwhile to tell.

Agents should have the freedom to work for days or weeks without producing anything conclusive. Reports on minor rules infractions and other petty irregularities should be discouraged. Such time-wasters can be avoided by limiting reports to the specific objectives of the agent's assignment. This procedure saves paper, hours, and money and, more important, focuses on the main tasks—finding the thieves and discovering loopholes in the restaurant's security system.

Secrecy of Reports

One sure way agents "blow their cover" is by being careless when they write their reports. They should never write anything in the presence of another person. If agents mail their reports, the return address should be a post office box or some other prearranged address. It is too easy for an employee to connect the agent with a home or work address. Agents should not make reports in person to employers. If an emergency arises that calls for a personal report, employer and agent should have a prearranged scenario in the event they are observed by a suspect or other employee.

When agents use a telephone for reporting, they should call at other than regular working hours and should use a pay phone at a distance from the restaurant. Managers should receive such calls directly and be able to speak in privacy. Home telephone contact is even safer if urgency is not a factor.

An agent pretending to work in collusion with dishonest employees is in a delicate situation. For the agent's protection, it might be wise for management to arrange a schedule for the agent to telephone in a report. If the agent is working under risk, the lack of a report at the scheduled time alerts management that something may be wrong and the agent may need immediate help.

Managers have to deal with confronting suspects when detectives or others provide evidence of internal theft in a facility.

8

Employee Questioning

Special Skills Are Needed

Managers need special communication skills to deal with employees who are suspected of theft. When dishonest employees are presented with evidence of their misconduct, they often lie, become aggressive, or react emotionally in some other way.

Some restaurants have training seminars to teach managers how to deal with problem situations. Typically, the managers are taught to stay calm, use effective communication techniques, present the evidence of misconduct without being overly accusatory, and ensure that they do not violate the employee's rights in any way. Other restaurants have specially trained security personnel, rather than managers, handle all questioning relating to theft incidents.

No matter who is responsible for questioning suspected employees, the goal of questioning is to identify those who are dishonest and determine how the restaurant might improve its supervision and control procedures to discourage further theft.

Inquiry Preparation

Before attempting to question suspected employees, questioners should ascertain whether or not larceny-theft can be proven. Larceny-theft means that something of value has been taken by a person with the intent to steal.

To prove a larceny-theft charge in a criminal court, the exact amount of money stolen or the specific cash value of items taken must be known and stated and there must be proof that the theft occurred. (See Part II on external theft for a more complete discussion of larceny-theft.)

Before meeting with suspects, questioners should know the answers to the following questions:

- Do we have all the facts regarding the case? Are there enough data to warrant an investigation? Is the information reliable, or are we dealing with suspicions or rumors? If the employee denies stealing, do we have evidence to counter claims of innocence and to prove the theft in a court of law? (Remember that if the employee does not confess, the restaurant may have to prosecute and prove the case in court.)

- Do we know as much as possible about the employee? Have we reviewed the suspect's employment card? Are there any time gaps in the employee's work record? Who are the employee's references? Are any of them employees of our restaurant? (These names will be important if the suspect is questioned later about collusion or knowledge of other dishonest employees.) Did the suspect's former company give a good recommendation? Have we telephoned the company to uncover information useful for the questioning?

- After reading all the reports in the case, did we take the time to interview the undercover agent, the employee who gave the incriminating information, or other sources of the charges? Do we know exactly what occurred? Are we familiar with the situation surrounding the reported theft? What time of day did it take place? Where was the person who reported the crime standing? What aspect of the situation first drew this person's attention?

- If the reported theft involves manipulation of company records, are we sure we understand the nature of the manipulation? What documents were changed? How, when, where, and by whom were they changed? Were documents rewritten or altered in other ways?

- Have we questioned the person who reported the alleged theft to be sure the witness saw and reported exactly what happened? Might the person have any ulterior motive for making such a report? (It is unusual for employees to come forward with information about other employees who are stealing, so it is wise not to jump to conclusions when an employee produces such evidence.) Do we have a method to check the reliability and validity of the evidence? Do we have a written, dated, signed, and witnessed statement in the handwriting of the accuser?

Before beginning an inquiry, a questioner must have all available details of the alleged theft. Because such situations are so serious, questioners should take their time in proceeding. To increase the chances of having a successful inquiry, it is best to delay the session until the necessary research has been completed.

Those who conduct the inquiry should be certain that only personnel who are directly involved in the investigation or people who have information to contribute to it are present at the meeting. If a questioner allows uninvited persons to listen to the conversation or to be present during questioning, charges of slander and defamation of character against the restaurant may result.

Emotional Readiness

Confronting employees with an accusation of theft is a difficult emotional experience for managers or other personnel who act as questioners. This is especially true if the questioners know the employees personally and believe them to be honest. Those conducting an inquiry may experience:

- Nervousness created by natural stress.

- A desire to rush through the interview to get the unpleasantness out of the way.

- A lack of self-confidence in the ability to handle the procedure.

- Emotional concern and sympathy for the suspect, but also anger at being betrayed by a previously trusted employee.

How to Conduct an Inquiry

Questioners who can establish a rapport with suspected employees and use sympathetic questioning techniques during an inquiry are most effective. Questioners must communicate an attitude of understanding during an inquiry even if they disapprove of or disagree with the employee's point of view and actions.

Fear tactics by questioners can cause suspects to panic and prevent them from being able to respond to questions. Furthermore, using excessive pressure in questioning employees is illegal.

Notifying Employees of an Inquiry

After managers or other questioners have decided to confront an employee, they must use care in how they notify the employee of the inquiry. It is best if an employee voluntarily comes to the meeting without knowing its purpose. When questioners casually handle an employee's invitation to the office, it can calm even a wary employee's fears and encourage the employee to participate.

Keeping the Door Unlocked

When an employee arrives at an inquiry, questioners must be sure that the suspect is treated in a lawful way. Interviewers must be aware of the balance between privacy and enforced confinement. It is appropriate for an employee to be questioned privately to protect both the employee and the restaurant. However, if the inquiry is conducted in a room with the door closed, the door must not be locked, and the employee must be aware that it is not locked.

Whenever possible, theft inquiries should be conducted during operating hours. This is more natural and arouses less suspicion. If after-hours questioning is unavoidable, more than one person should be in the room to ensure that the questioner is protected from any charges of abuse, improper advances, or misconduct. If the employee being questioned is a woman, a female executive of the restaurant should be present during the inquiry.

Suspects can sue the facility for false imprisonment if they are held against their will. To protect the restaurant from costly legal suits, questioners should tell the employee, upon reaching the point of asking about actual thefts, that any further discussion of the problem is on a voluntary basis and that the employee should feel free to end the discussion and leave at any time.

Taping the Inquiry

Some companies, after informing the suspect, tape record theft inquiries. Although they are not admissable in a court of law, recordings can be important if the subject makes a verbal confession and later refuses to sign a written statement. Tape recordings protect questioners from future charges of abusive tactics or of threats and promises to persuade the suspect to confess. Another benefit of a tape recording is that questioners who must appear in court can easily refresh their memories of the inquiry by listening to the tape.

Tapes containing both successful and unsuccessful inquiries can be kept in a tape library and used as a training tool. They can help questioners improve their interviewing skills.

Opening the Inquiry

An inquiry should begin with small talk—some basic questions about the employee's interests. To avoid emotional strain, questioners should not address such topics as an employee's social life or other personal things that might trigger an undesirable response. Questions that start with "how" or "why" are generally more effective, since they encourage the subject to talk.

Questioners must remember that the purpose of an inquiry is to encourage subjects to talk about themselves. Subjects may be lonely, frightened, puzzled, or disturbed persons. They generally respond favorably when questioners show they have a genuine interest in them.

If employees press to discuss the real purpose of the inquiry, the questioner can stall by saying, "We'll get around to that in a minute, but first I'd like to talk a little more about you." Under no circumstances should questioners allow employees to force them into a premature introduction of the theft problem.

Obtaining Feedback

After a few minutes of conversation, questioners may be able to encourage the suspect to reflect upon personal problems and express true feelings. Here again, it is important for questioners to be perceived as concerned and genuinely interested in the employee.

When it's time to discuss the crime, questioners can proceed carefully and gradually with a statement such as, "We have noticed some problems lately concerning the failure of the cash register to balance properly when it is checked. You have had a series of cash shortages recently, and we wonder if perhaps you had some explanation." If the employee does not have an immediate explanation to offer, questioners can press for information on how the employee handled the register on days when the shortages occurred.

Handling Admissions of Guilt

If questioners have succeeded in building a good relationship with the subject, it is likely the subject will accept the questioners' suggestion to provide information. To prosecute the suspect, questioners must obtain as much information as possible. At the same time, however, questioners need to be humane and help the employee face the situation.

To conduct an effective inquiry, questioners should treat the suspect with dignity and attempt to make the inquiry as nonthreatening as possible. Every effort should be made to convince the employee that a clear conscience is worthwhile.

Questioners must use language that is conducive to getting an employee to cooperate. Words such as "steal" or "thief" will produce hostile responses, while using the words "take" or "borrow" will keep the conversation going. Also, bluffing has no place in an inquiry. By attempting to fool suspects, questioners destroy their credibility.

Generally, questioners do succeed in getting suspects to give the details of a theft. When suspects refuse to cooperate in an inquiry, questioners can say that they will turn the matter over to the proper authorities. By not using the word police, questioners can avoid creating a threatening situation which might impair a suspect's ability to respond.

Whether or not they are successful in getting an employee to admit to a theft, questioners must maintain the proper perspective in an inquiry and adhere to all company theft inquiry policies and procedures.

Although store security personnel are not required to, a regular policeman working part-time as a security officer should give the Miranda warning.

A Written Statement

If a suspected employee admits to a theft, it is preferable to have the suspect make a written statement in as much detail as possible, including specific incidents, methods, and amounts of money involved or value of the items stolen. The written statement should be in the suspect's own handwriting, as it is a stronger piece of evidence if criminal charges are going to be pressed. This also helps to protect the store from possible charges of extortion or blackmail by the suspect who feels that he or she was unduly pressured into making a confession.

Management must decide if they are going to press criminal charges or merely demand financial restitution, or both. If the written statement has in it an agreement for financial restitution, the crime committed has been turned into a debt and the suspect cannot be charged with a criminal offense. The restitution agreed upon can only be enforced through civil court.

After the statement has been written, the employee should read it aloud. Then the questioners should ask if the employee understands everything in it or wishes to make any changes. If changes are requested by the suspect, questioners should request that the suspect ink in the corrections and initial them. Then the suspect should write, "I have written and read this statement and it is true to the best of my knowledge," and should sign the statement (name, address, and date). If there are several pages to the document, the employee should sign every page. Next, two witnesses should sign. The time at which the employee enters and leaves the inquiry should be noted. If the police have been contacted, the time at which the police were notified and the time they arrived at the facility should be noted on the document. The names of all questioners and others at the inquiry should be written on the document as well.

Ending the Inquiry

At the end of the session, questioners should be especially alert to the mental state of the employee. They may need to escort the employee home or call members of the employee's family for assistance. Unfortunately, security files include tragic accounts of emotionally disturbed employees who were allowed to leave inquiries alone. In some cases, young people have run away from home; in others, individuals have injured themselves or even attempted suicide.

After the employee has left the facility, those who conducted the inquiry should write a summary of the interview. It should contain the method of theft, why the employee started stealing, when the stealing began, and any other pertinent information. Such a summary cannot be introduced as evidence in a court of law, but it can be used as a reference by those who conducted the inquiry.

Dealing with the Consequences

Restaurateurs face the difficult decision of what actions to take against a previously trusted, highly capable, long-time employee who is caught stealing. Not only are managers likely to be shocked to discover that the person is stealing, but they may also feel that the theft is out of character for that person. Is it wise to give the person a second chance?

The answer is an emphatic *no.* The person should not be retained, regardless of the circumstances that led to the incident. Continuing to employ a thief has a contaminating influence on honest employees. Co-workers who see that a thief has been kept on the payroll can be so angry with the restaurant's management that they themselves begin to steal as an attempt at revenge.

A restaurateur can terminate an employee for dishonesty, a police violation, company policy violation, or a larceny prosecution. However, doing so should be handled as humanely as possible, considering how devastating an experience termination can be.

Part II

The External Dimension

Part I of this text has examined internal theft—what it is, how it occurs, and how to prevent it. Dishonest employees steal when they have a motive, are given an opportunity, and can rationalize their actions. These same theft determinants also lead to other types of criminal acts perpetrated by those outside the restaurant. Part II looks at the nature of external crime, how it can affect restaurants, and what can be done to deter criminals.

9

Robbery and Burglary

Restaurants Are a Target

Restaurants are becoming targets for non-residential robbery and burglary. They are vulnerable to theft because of their locations near major roadways, late-night operating hours, and their lack of security systems.

Robbery differs from burglary. According to the United States Department of Justice, an event designated a nonresidential robbery entails "force or threat of force to take or attempt to take money, merchandise, equipment, or supplies [from people] whether or not the offender has a weapon." (13) Two elements are necessary to consider an act robbery:

- **There must be a victim present.** Property must be taken either directly from a person or in a person's presence. Taking property from an empty room may be burglary or other type of theft, but is not considered robbery.

- **The victim must be threatened or be**

89

subjected to some type of force or other violence. The force used to take or retain possession of stolen property must be actual, not inferred.

If no use of force or violence exists, the crime is considered larceny-theft. This is defined by the Justice Department as "the unlawful taking, carrying, leading, or riding away of property from the possession or constrictive possession of another." (13)

Robberies are classified according to what is used: firearms; knives or other cutting instruments; other dangerous weapons (such as clubs, lead pipes, brass knuckles, acids, and explosives); or strong-arm tactics.

Robbery Statistics

Each year, an estimated half-million robberies are committed in this country. Twelve percent of these, or approximately 60,000 robberies, occur in commercial facilities (nonresidential buildings other than banks, gas stations, or convenience stores). Total robbery losses are $313 million each year and average $628 per incident. (9) Average losses for commercial facilities are even higher—the average loss is about $991. (13) "An estimated 52 restaurants are robbed daily in the United States," (7) and robbery losses from fast-service restaurants alone total about $9 million each year. (8)

Restaurants suffer more than monetary losses because of robberies. One-third of all robbery victims in the U.S. are injured. Strong-arm tactics are used in 42 percent of all robberies; firearms are used in 35 percent; knives and other cutting instruments are used in 13 percent; and other types of weapons are used for the remainder. (9)

Robberies are not geographically confined—they occur throughout the country. The latest available government figures reveal that 34 percent of robberies were committed in southern states; 30 percent in western states; 19 percent in midwestern states; and 17 percent in northern states. (9)

Robbery rates are highest in well-populated areas. Statistics show that cities of over 1 million people suffered 965 robberies per 100,000 people, compared to 266 robberies per 100,000 people in metropolitan areas; 44 robberies per 100,000 people in cities outside metropolitan areas; and 15 robberies per 100,000 people in rural areas. (9)

Although robberies can occur anytime people are present in a facility, they are frequently committed:

- During fall and winter months when it is easier for robbers to hide weapons under jackets, coats, or other bulky clothes. Robbery rates are generally higher in December and lower in April.

- Between 8 p.m. and 2 a.m. (12)

- When a facility first opens or is about to close, or at other times when there are few guests present.

- At the end of high-volume days or at other times when facilities have large amounts of cash on hand.

A Robber's Characteristics

Typically, robberies are committed by young men. Ninety-two percent of the people arrested for robbery in a given year are male and 65 percent are under 25 years old. (9) Criminal justice employees classify robbers as either amateur or professional. Amateur robbers usually work alone, are unarmed, and have no criminal record. They tend to "commit robberies with little or no planning; take great risks for relatively small amounts of money; and tend to be more violent than professional robbers." (10) Most professional robbers have criminal records, work in groups, and are armed. They are less likely to act impulsively. They plan their robberies and tend to follow a pattern in committing them.

Despite their media image, robbers seldom wear disguises except for sunglasses and/or hats to conceal their eye and hair color. All robbers, regardless of their appearance, "must be considered dangerous and capable of committing assault, kidnapping, or murder to accomplish their objectives of robbery and escape." (10)

Types of Robberies

Restaurants are susceptible to several types of robberies. Managers or other employees can be robbed while taking funds to or from the bank, or robbers can enter the facility and demand that employees give them money from cash registers, cash rooms, and/or safes. "Robberies of deposits and cash registers are more frequent than robberies of safes," (12) but robberies of safes are usually more dangerous because they take longer and can entail hostage taking.

How Targets Are Chosen

Most robbers choose their targets carefully. They look for careless operating procedures or other gaps in a restaurant's security system. Professional robbers look for targets with the following characteristics:

- **Convenient locations.** Restaurants located in areas with good escape routes are more likely to be robbed. Since most fast-service operations are located on main roads or near highways, "They are particularly vulnerable to robbery because their locations enable a fast getaway. Restaurants in shopping centers and at busy street locations suffer less robbery and vandalism than do freestanding or remote buildings." (8) Also preferred by robbers are restaurants that are free from barriers such as construction equipment and traffic lights.

- **Lack of police surveillance.** Restaurants located near police stations, along patrol routes, or those patronized by police officers are less likely to be robbed. (10)

- **Poor physical security.** Robbers inspect the areas surrounding a facility. Poorly lighted parking lots and walkways, unlocked back doors, and unsecured windows invite crime. Robbers also check the inside of a facility. They may loiter in the facility, claiming they are waiting for someone, or they may try to inspect non-guest areas (such as cash rooms and supply areas) by pretending to look for the manager's office so they can apply for a job. Once in the facility they look for alarms and other security devices, the location of the cash room and safe, and possible escape routes.

- **Lack of effective operating procedures.** Robbers observe opening and closing procedures. They look for restaurants that have only one or two employees present during these times and for facilities that keep all doors unlocked until closing. They also observe cash-handling procedures by dining in the restaurant and paying for their meal with a large denomination bill. In this way, they can estimate the amount of money kept on hand for changemaking. They also look for facilities where:

   Cashiers turn their backs on guests or leave cash drawers unattended.

   Cash is visibly taken from registers to cash rooms or safes.

   Cash is counted in unlocked back rooms or in guest areas.

   Robbers also observe deposit procedures and assess whether or not there is a pattern to how deposits are made. Their job is made easier when restaurants send the same person to the bank at the same time on specified days, using the same route.

Burglary Defined

The Justice Department states a nonresidential burglary has occurred when "the offender tried to get into the building illegally; and there was evidence that the offender used force to get in; or the offender actually got into the building with or without using force." (13) Burglaries are classified as:

- **Forcible entry.** In addition to incidents where force is used to enter the facility, this also refers to incidents where the burglar lawfully enters the facility before closing, hides until the facility has closed, and then leaves the facility either before or after it is opened by employees.

- **Unlawful entry without force.** The burglar enters the facility through an unlocked door or window.

- **Attempted forcible entry.** This includes uncompleted robberies where force was used to gain entry.

Burglary Statistics

There are an estimated three million burglaries a year. One-third of these burglaries are in nonresidential properties. Seventy percent of all burglaries are forcible entry, 22 percent are entry without force, and 8 percent are attempted forcible entries. (9)

Burglary losses total about $3 billion each year and average $913 per nonresidential occurrence. Thirty-seven percent of burglaries were in southern states, followed by 26 percent, 21 percent, and 17 percent in western, midwestern, and northeastern states, respectively. Burglaries take place most frequently in August, and least often in February. (9)

Like robbers, the majority of burglars are young men. Ninety-three percent of arrested burglars in a given year were men, 73 percent of whom were under 25 years of age. Most arrested burglars were convicted of their crimes; only 14 percent were cleared. (9)

Burglary Techniques

Burglars may steal cash or merchandise from restaurants. They observe facilities during business hours for a few days before the crime. They note the habits of owners, managers, employees, neighborhood residents, and police officers, and determine if the facility has alarms or other security systems. Burglars gain access to restaurants by:

- **Entering the facility before closing.** Burglars can hide until the building has been locked and the last employee has left. They may exit the building immediately after the theft or hide until the facility reopens.

- **Entering through a door, window, wall, or ceiling opening.** Burglars can gain admittance through unlocked or otherwise unsecured doors or windows, rooftop doors, fire escapes, or skylights. Or, they jimmy doors, smash windows, or drill a hole in a wall or ceiling of the facility. Sometimes they enter an adjacent building and drill or cut a hole through a common wall.

Prevention Is the Key

Robberies and burglaries are more likely to occur when there are weaknesses in the restaurant's security system—either in defective policies and procedures or in the physical facility. To optimally protect the physical operation, it is essential to examine the premises to identify, then secure, any vulnerable areas. These are often doors, windows, or other possible entries, or spaces with inadequate lighting.

Doors

The vulnerable points on a door include not only its locks, but also its frame, hinges, and panels. Doors need to fit securely into frames. A crowbar or other device can be used to pry open a door if there is a one-quarter inch or wider gap. (10) Frames need to be inspected regularly for rotting and looseness.

Secure hinges are either on the inside of the door or are concealed. When they must face outward, hinges should be installed so that the screws cannot be removed and they can withstand manipulations with a chisel or similar tool. Hinge pins welded to the hinges provide added protection.

The most secure door panels are made from steel or solid wood. Wood panels can be reinforced with crossbars or with heavy sheet metal plates attached to the inside of the door. If doors have glass panels, bars or grills (screens) are necessary to prevent burglars from breaking the glass to gain access to the building. Wire screens or bars on glass areas should be spaced no more than five inches apart. They must also be made from materials that resist illegal entry. Steel screens should contain at least one-eighth inch material and two-inch mesh. The diameter of round bars should be at least one-half inch; one-inch wide and one-quarter-inch thick are desirable for flat bars. Screens and bars can be secured with roundhead flush bolts.

Rear, side, and other doors not used by guests also need protection. The most secure ones are constructed from solid metal. Rolling or overhead receiving doors not controlled or locked by electric power should be protected with slide bolts on the bottom bar. Chain-operated overhead doors can be secured with a cast iron keeper and pin.

Solid, overhead, swinging, sliding, or accordion-type doors should be secured with a metal crossbar on the inside. Metal or grill-type accordion doors can be inserted into a secure metal guide track at both bottom and top for added protection. In addition, a cylinder lock or padlock can be used.

Naturally, doors must be locked when not in use. One fast-service restaurant "locks doors to its dining room at midnight on Friday and Saturday nights, with only drive-through service available until the 2 a.m. closing. During the week, the back dining room doors are locked at 9 p.m. After that time, guests must enter by the counter doors where they can be easily seen." (8)

Since robbers often enter through back or kitchen doors, these doors require extra security. Employees should never prop these doors open (even when they are receiving a delivery or taking out the garbage). Some facilities recommend that employees not use these doors after dark.

Areas surrounding doors also require attention. Shrubs, dark areas, and garbage cans are potential hiding places. Keeping entries well-lighted and ensuring that shrubs are too low to hide behind help deter criminals.

Windows

Burglars often enter facilities through rear or other sheltered-from-view windows. Windows that can be opened should be secured on the inside with a bolt, crossbar, or lock. The frame of the window should be securely fastened to the building so it cannot be pried, freeing the entire window. Since window panes, like glass door panels, can be broken or cut out, bars or grills can be installed on the inside and welded to the frame or secured so they cannot be released with a crowbar. Outside hinges on a window should not contain removable pins; these can be welded, flanged, or otherwise secured. To provide maximum security, many operators substitute glass brick, which is difficult to penetrate, in a window not needed for ventilation. Naturally, all fire-code regulations must be taken into account when securing any entry or exit.

It cannot be assumed that even high windows are secure. Often, these can be reached from the roof of another building, a tree, or a fire escape. Transom windows also require attention. Since transoms are wide enough to allow a person to enter, they should be secured.

Bulletproof windows are installed by some operators for added security and are used for drive-through windows by some fast-service operators (8).

Other Entries

In addition to doors and windows, other areas of the facility must be protected. "If burglars know your doors and windows are wired, they will look for other ways to gain access," such as: (4)

- **Manholes.** Manholes used for heat, gas, and water pipes provide access to a building. The manhole cover of a tunnel that leads to the interior of the facility can be secured with a chain and padlock or combination lock to eliminate unauthorized use.

- **Gratings.** Some restaurants have steel gratings at ground level to provide convenient access to the basement. Although they seem to offer good protection because they are of strong construction and look solid, gratings are not always adequately fastened to their frames. Frames must be properly secured and grates welded into place or fastened with a chain and lock. As with other openings, gratings require periodic security inspections.

- **Roofs.** Some restaurateurs fail to secure roof areas. Doors to the roof provide access to the building, and because they are used infrequently, are often overlooked. These entrances can be reinforced with locks, bars, or chains and should be inspected regularly to ensure that they have not been left unsecured after use. Skylights can be protected in the same way as windows—with bars and screens. Skylights that do not need to be opened should be sealed.

- **Ventilating shafts.** Some ventilating shafts are large enough to permit entrance into the facility. Burglars can remove ventilating fans or bend fan blades to make an opening wide enough for their bodies to fit through. Ventilating ducts should be secured with bars rather than screens, which can impede air flow.

- **Fire escapes.** Any door or opening leading to a fire escape must be secured, yet as with other entries and exits, remain in compliance with fire codes.

- **Walls.** Most walls are solidly constructed and are not used to gain illegal entry. However, it is possible for burglars to break through some walls, especially when they are in the basement or divide adjoining buildings.

Locks, Keys and Other Access Devices, and Alarms

Although these items are the obvious means to secure a facility, they are not all equally protective.

Locks

Although, "No door lock is pick-proof or absolutely unopenable," (13) locks are deterrents. Restaurateurs must evaluate available locks and choose those that are the best value to perform the necessary security function.

- **Warded locks.** A warded lock incorporates wards or obstructions inside the lock to prevent a key from moving the bolt unless the key has corresponding notches that permit it to pass these obstructions. A warded lock has a simple construction and is easily picked. Warded locks are useful for interior doors to ensure employee privacy, but are not recommended for security purposes.

- **Disc or wafer tumbler locks.** A disc tumbler lock contains flat metal discs with open centers cut in various lengths. Disc tumblers are fitted into a plug, which fits into a lock case. When locked, spring tension forces the discs partially out of the plug and into recesses or slots in the case, thus preventing the plug from turning the cylinder. When the proper key is inserted, all the tumblers are withdrawn allowing the plug to turn and to cause the movement of the bolt. This type of lock, like a warded lock, is rarely used for security purposes. It is not strong enough to resist jimmying or prevent break-ins.

- **Pin tumbler locks.** Pin tumbler locks are key-operated and fairly secure. They consist of an inner plug within an outer shell. Rotating the inner plug with a key moves the cam at the back of the cylinder and activates the lock mechanism. Several pins prevent the rotation of the plug when the cylinder is locked. Pin tumbler locks may be defeated by picking, taking an impression of the cylinder to manufacture a key, or by pulling the cylinder forcibly from the lock case. Pin tumblers with less than five pins should be avoided because they can be picked easily.

- **Padlocks.** Padlocks are often used to join a chain or chains and are installed in conjunction with a hasp. The hasp must be of high quality and made from material that is as heavy and as strong as the padlock itself. How the hasp is installed affects the strength of the padlock. The hasp should be mounted so it is difficult to remove. When the hasp is attached to metal, it must be welded. Since ordinary screws can be pried, strong bolts with washers are usually used. When choosing padlocks, it is important to inspect the locking mechanism and shackle. Light locking mechanisms can spring open when the padlock is hit with a hammer or other blunt instrument, and shackles made of soft steel or brass are easily sawed.

- **Combination locks.** A combination lock is usually more secure than other types of locks because there is no access to its inner parts. However, a well-constructed lever or pin tumbler lock takes more time to pick than an inexpensive combination lock.

- **Magnetic locks.** Magnetic locks use the principles of magnetic attraction and repulsion. The tumblers consist of a series of magnets with different polarities arranged in a variety of angles within the cylinder. Corresponding magnets concealed within the body of a cylindrical key activate the magnetic tumblers to release the plug and permit the locking mechanism to move. When the key is removed, a repelling force from the fixed magnets in the cylinder automatically returns the magnetic tumblers to the locked position. The mechanism is designed so that the key cannot be removed from the lock until it is fully locked. Since the key is magnetic and has no teeth, no impression can be made. Locks are individually keyed so that keys cannot be duplicated without reference to magnetic codes controlled by the manufacturer. Magnetic locks must be carefully chosen, since some models can be opened with a strong magnet.

- **Electronic locks.** An electronic lock is operated by a code card, which, when inserted into a slot in the lock, activates it. Other electronic locks are activated by pushing a series of buttons on the surface of the lock.

Since most locks can either be picked or forced open with a crowbar, it is necessary to reinforce them. Lock cylinders can be forced open by using pliers, a pipe wrench, or other grabbing device to twist the cylinder out of the door, leaving an opening through which the dead bolt or latch bolt can be removed. This can be prevented by installing a case-hardened steel ring around the cylinder.

Case-hardened bolts provide additional security against the cutting of a latch bolt or dead bolt. Alternatively, hard steel rods or roller bearings can be attached to the bolt to cause it to revolve freely if it is sawed.

To provide full protection, locks must be inspected regularly and cases must be checked for signs of wear or other damage. A competent locksmith should check the locking mechanisms.

Keys, Combinations, and Control Cards

Even the best locks provide little protection if restaurant operators fail to control the distribution and use of keys, combinations, or control cards. Too often, an operator provides these to all employees for the sake of convenience. Good control means taking the following precautions:

- **Restrict distribution.** Issue as few keys, combinations, or control cards as possible.

- **Keep up-to-date, accurate records.** Records indicating the location of each lock, the names of employees who have access, and the date that each key, combination, or control card was issued are important for proper control.

- **Prevent unauthorized duplication.** Use keys stamped "Do Not Duplicate" and control cards that are difficult to forge. Instruct employees to keep their keys in their possession at all times. Keys are never to be given to other people, or left in locks, in locker rooms, on desks, or given to parking attendants.

- **Re-key or re-code when necessary.** Locks need to be re-keyed or re-coded when an employee leaves the company without handing in keys and when keys are reported lost or stolen.

- **Avoid using master keys.** Few employees need keys to all secured areas. Although master keys are convenient, they weaken a facility's security system.

- **Use codes to identify keys and control cards.** Only authorized personnel should know how to determine which lock a particular key or control card fits. Keys should never contain the restaurant's name, address, or telephone number.

- **Store extra keys or cards carefully.** Spares must be kept in a locked area.

- **Inventory keys and control cards.** Operators should conduct audits of the keys and control cards issued to employees. An audit provides physical verification that employees have the items they were issued, and that none have been loaned, lost, or stolen.

- **Use the services of a qualified locksmith.** Reputable, licensed locksmiths can provide information on the proper locks to use, as well as install locks, cut keys, and make necessary repairs.

Alarms

Alarm systems have two purposes: to detect an intruder and to act as a psychological deterrent. Effective alarm systems cover "all possible points of entry . . . including doors, windows, skylights, ceilings, and—especially if the (building) . . . is of cinderblock construction or adjoins other buildings—the walls." (1) Alarm systems use various operating principles to spot intruders. These include systems that detect:

- **A break in an electrical circuit.** These alarms typically consist of a sensing device through which a continuous current flows. The alarm is activated when there is a break in the current.

- **Interruption of a light beam.** A beam is directed from a sending device to a receiving cell, causing a continuous beam. If the beam is interrupted, such as when a person walks through the beam, an alarm is activated. Electric-eye systems are effective, since they emit an invisible, infrared beam (1).

- **Sounds, vibrations, or motion.** Ultrasonic or sonic detectors respond to sounds in the facility. These types of devices "use high-frequency waves and trigger the alarm when the waves are interrupted by a preset amount of air turbulence, created by the movement within the [facility] . . . Sonic detectors use low-frequency waves which trigger the alarm when an actual noise bounces off the radio waves." (1) Motion can also be detected with radar or stress units. These units detect movement in the area of transmission.

- **Variations in electric or magnetic fields.** These alarms are often called "proximity devices" or "capacity alarms." They sound whenever a foreign body disturbs either an electrical or magnetic field. These systems are typically used to protect cash rooms or the area surrounding a safe.

Alarm System Connections

An alarm is only effective if it is heard and a response is made. Alarms can register on-site or be connected to a police station or private alarm company.

- **On-site alarms.** On-site (or local) alarms sound a bell, gong, or siren at the facility to frighten intruders. These alarms rarely assist in capturing intruders, because there is time for them to flee before alarm company personnel or the police arrive.

- **Police station alarms.** "The best alarm is a silent system that is connected to the police department or a private security system. It can detect a break-in, fire, loud noises, or unauthorized entry with a key." (4) Other types of silent alarms incorporate "panic buttons" which can be activated to inform police that a robbery is in progress. In addition to installing panic buttons in the cash room, foot- or knee-activated buttons are often placed near cash registers. (4)

- **Private alarm companies.** Alarm systems that sound at an alarm or other private company are effective. Typically, alarm company personnel respond to the alarm, inform the restaurant owner and/or manager, and notify the police. Like police station alarms, these systems are more effective than alarm systems that sound solely at the restaurant.

Lighting as a Crime Deterrent

When it comes to safety and security, lighting has a dual purpose. It helps prevent accidents by making people aware of obstacles, and it is also a shield against intruders. Lighted areas make a criminal think twice before attempting to enter an establishment.

A restaurant needs effective lighting inside and outside. Contrast and brightness should be balanced so that the exterior of the restaurant is illuminated, but the inside of the establishment can still be seen. To deter crime, the entire exterior of the facility, including parking lots, pathways, and doors, must be well-lighted. Light fixtures must be positioned to avoid glare and shadows. Areas that can serve as hiding places, such as behind stairs, ramps, shrubs, fountains, or fences should also be illuminated.

Interior lighting controls should be positioned so the first employees who enter the facility when it opens can create a lighting pathway as they proceed from one area to the next. Employees should not have to pass through dark areas (where intruders can lurk) to reach control panels.

Lighting control panels must be protected so they cannot be tampered with. Company employees need written procedures describing what they should do to safeguard guests and secure the premises if lights in the restaurant go out because of tampering, blackouts, or any other reason. Even a momentary blackout is a security concern.

Supplementing Public Police Protection

Some facilities hire security employees or use personnel supplied by private security agencies to supplement public police protection. Usually, such personnel are responsible for:

- Patrolling the premises to prevent, detect, or investigate the presence of intruders.

- Conducting security checks to make sure employees are following all security procedures.

- Notifying facility owners and managers when security problems are discovered.

- Working with law enforcement agents in the investigation of crimes in the facility.

- Attesting to a facility's security conditions before, during, and after a crime to expedite insurance claims or deal with legal matters.

Although some companies hire armed security personnel, "the evidence is that armed guards escalate violence. . . The presence of armed guards may cause exchanges of gunfire between guards and robbers in which employees and customers may be injured." (8)

Employees Have an Important Role

Well-trained employees who carry out carefully designed security policies and procedures can be the best deterrent to crime in the restaurant. "Policies and procedures should be set by . . . management and followed scrupulously since these are both sound business practices and the best way to maintain (security system) integrity." (1)

Opening and Closing Procedures

Since opening and closing times are high risk periods where robbery is concerned, extra precautions must be taken as follows:

- **Permit no employee to open or close the restaurant alone.**

- **Instruct employees that before opening doors they should drive around the exterior of the building to inspect for signs of entry, damage, or the presence of unfamiliar cars or people.** If they feel anything is suspicious, they should use a telephone away from the premises to contact the police. (It is wise for those who open and close facilities to always carry the telephone number of the police department and sufficient change to make a call.)

- **Use the front or other obvious door for entry or final exit.** Employees are less likely to be attacked when they use doors that are visible from the street.

- **Have one employee wait outside while another inspects the facility.** The employee waiting outside should contact police if the employee checking the facility does not return to the door within a given period.

- **Keep all doors locked until opening for business and admit only scheduled employees.**

- **Lock customer doors at closing time, and have a designated employee stationed at one door to unlock it to allow guests to exit.** Keys should never be left in the door for any reason.

- **Admit no one into the facility after closing.** "No customer or unknown person should be allowed to re-enter . . . after closing for any reason, including alleged car trouble, etc. If any person has trouble with his or her vehicle and has missed the bus, etc., talk to the person without opening the door, and offer to contact someone by telephone to assist the person." (10)

- **Inspect the entire restaurant before closing to ensure that no one is hiding.** This includes locker rooms, restrooms, and storage areas.

- **Check outside areas before leaving the building.** Employees should remain in the facility until no one is on the grounds. Police should be notified if there are suspicious loiterers on the premises. (3)

Managers or other employees must be wary of telephone calls they receive at home in which they are asked to return to a facility after it has closed. If callers claim to represent service, delivery, or other companies needing emergency access, employees should verify the request by calling the company in question. Calls that prove to be a hoax should be reported to the facility's security force or the police.

Cash Handling Procedures

"A successful robbery prevention program must be based on good cash reduction techniques. The less money available to a would-be robber the better." (12) Operators can post signs on doors and at registers stating that a limited amount of funds is kept in the facility. (3) In addition, restaurants should never publicize sales, deposit amounts, or any other information related to the amount of money taken in at the facility. (12)

Controlling funds at the register, in the cash room, and while making deposits is also important. Charts 9.1, 9.2, and 9.3 list cash control techniques at these points.

Employee Behavior

How employees behave can affect whether or not a crime will be attempted. Employees should acknowledge every guest who enters the restaurant. A greeting is a form of attention that deters a would-be robber. During a greeting, employees have the opportunity to "size up" a guest and note behavior that isn't quite right.

Handling A Robbery

Unfortunately, robberies do occur. During a robbery, the safety of personnel and guests is the primary consideration. Proper employee training is necessary to emphasize not only the correct procedures to

---

Chart 9.1. Cash Handling Procedures at Cash Registers

- Position registers so cashiers face guests at all times.

- Place registers on wide counters so robbers cannot reach into the register, take money, and run.

- Mark several bills, record the serial numbers, and place the bills at the bottom of their respective stacks. Do not give these bills out as change. If the facility is robbed, the cashier can give these bills to the robber, thus aiding in identification.

- Keep large denomination bills and travelers checks under the cash drawer as robbers may ignore them.

- Stamp all checks "For Deposit Only" as soon as they are received. If held up, a few checks can be placed in cash bags along with money, thus aiding in identification of robbers.

- Keep completed credit card receipts in a separate box located under the counter. If these are stolen with the cash, the facility will have no way to collect on them.

- Don't allow funds to accumulate. Make regular deposits from registers to cash rooms. Be discreet when moving funds in the facility.

- Keep empty registers open after closing. This shows would-be burglars that drawers are empty, and there is no money in the facility.

Source: (3, 4, 11, 12).

---

follow during and after a robbery, but the importance of remaining calm and composed. Chart 9.4 lists employee behavioral guidelines to follow during a robbery, and Chart 9.5 lists procedures for employees to follow after a robbery has occurred.

Investigating Occurrences of Robbery and Burglary

Catching robbers after they have left a crime scene is extraordinarily difficult. Police must gather information from witnesses, examine the scene of the robbery, and compare the details of the robbery with other

---

Chart 9.2. Cash Control Techniques in the Cash Room

- Locate cash room in a secure area. The cash room should be located in the interior of the facility. None of its walls should be on the perimeter of the building. The room should never have a window or an opening to the outside. Cash rooms should never share a common wall with another building.

- Don't label cash room doors.

- Keep cash room doors locked. "The counting or office area where the safe is located should be equipped with a dead-bolt lock (1" throw) and a peephole or other observational device." (12)

- Use safes for added security. Burglar-resistant safes should be used. In addition:

  Keep safes out of guest view.

  Restrict the combination to managers and authorized employees.

  Place funds in the safe immediately after counting them.

  Use safes with drop chutes. "Ideally the safe should be designed so that cashiers and others who make deposit drops or return funds after use, do so into a drop chute into a separate section of the safe." (12) Some newer safes function as safes and money machines. One company has a "cash controller [which] functions both as a safe where employees can drop large bills and as a money machine that will vend only $15 in cash at a time. The time delay of 2 to 10 minutes between vending takes advantage of the fact that most robberies are completed in a minute or less." (8)

Source: (8, 12).

---

robberies in an effort to identify a robber's pattern. As one security expert explained, "It's a sad commentary on the present status of law enforcement, but unless you have a shooting victim or some solid identification your chances of apprehending a robber are remote. Police readily admit that unless they catch a person in the act or carrying the money, the chances of apprehension and identification—let alone prosecution—are practically nil." (4)

Chart 9.3. Cash Control While Making Deposits

- When taking money to and from the bank, be unpredictable. The time of day, the route, and the method of concealing the cash should vary.

- Don't allow funds to accumulate. Make timely deposits.

- Record some cash serial numbers when making deposits.

- Make banking hour deposits at a teller's window if possible. Use automatic teller machines (ATMs) and bank depository slots only when the only other alternative is to leave cash sitting in the facility.

- Disguise money when transporting it. While some operators have employees carry money in unmarked bags, briefcases, pocketbooks, or paper bags, it is safer to carry money in trouser or coat pockets.

- Only designated employees should transport funds, but the same employee should not make every deposit.

- Night deposits should be made by two employees. "One employee (if two cars are taken) should return to the unit ensuring that the drop has been made. If an employee fails to return from making a deposit, the police should be contacted." (12) For added safety, employees should drive around the bank and check for suspicious persons before getting out of their cars. Some operators make arrangements for security personnel to be at the bank when they must make night deposits.

Source: (1, 2, 11, 12).

Apprehending burglars can be even more difficult than catching robbers, especially when there are no witnesses. Burglary investigations often begin with an examination of the premises and employee interviews. Police typically ask for:

- Date and estimated time of burglary.

- Exact description of what was stolen.

- Statements from witnesses.

- Possible explanation of how a burglar could know where to find the money and or merchandise.

Chart 9.4. Employee Behavior During a Robbery

- Stay calm. When employees or guests get excited, robbers may panic and act impulsively.

- Cooperate. "Once a robbery has started, it's too late for the robber to back down, but it's not too late to get mad and harm someone. Don't argue, just cooperate." (6)

- Keep it short and smooth. The average robbery lasts less than two minutes, but the longer it takes, the more likely the robber will become nervous and harm someone. Treat the incident as though it were a normal guest transaction.

- Tell the robber about potential surprises. "If you [are going to] make a move, tell the robber first. If other employees (or guests) are in back (or elsewhere in the facility), tell the robber so he/she is not surprised if someone comes out." (12)

- Note as many details as possible. "Try to remember distinguishing features of the robber—clothing, scars, marks, weapon type, height, weight, hair color, and length. Remember what the robber says." (12) Some facilities mark exit door frames at 5'8", 6', and 6'2" to be able to gauge a robber's height. (4) Employees also need to note if robbers are wearing gloves, and what they touch. If robbers are not wearing gloves, the surfaces they touch can be checked for fingerprints.

- Do not play hero. No amount of money is worth the risk of injury or death. Proper cash handling procedures keep monetary losses to a minimum.

- Do not use a weapon. Employees should never be allowed to bring weapons to work.

- Activate an alarm or call the police as soon as robbers leave.

- Do not chase robbers. Stay in the facility. Robbers often shoot at pursuers, or police could mistake an employee for a robber.

Source: (3, 4, 5, 6, 10, 12).

Chart 9.5. Procedures to Follow After a Robbery

- Ask police for instructions, and follow their orders.

- Calm other employees and guests. Request that all witnesses remain in the facility until the police arrive. Do not let witnesses discuss the incident as this may result in an inaccurate description of the robbers.

- Have all witnesses fill out robber description forms (see Chart 9.6).

- Notify the manager or owner in accordance with company policy.

- Do not make statements to the press or others about the incident or amount of losses.

Source: (3, 5, 10, 12).

- A description of closing procedures and whether they were followed.

- The names or descriptions of possible suspects, such as discharged employees or people seen loitering near the facility within the past few days.

In case of substantial burglaries, investigators may look for evidence such as fingerprints, footprints, objects (such as tools) the burglars left behind, and any other clue to a burglar's identity.

Chart 9.6. Robbery Description Form

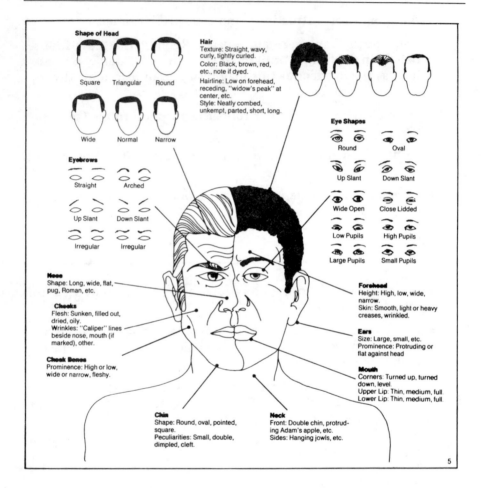

Shape of Head

Square   Triangular   Round

Wide   Normal   Narrow

Hair
Texture: Straight, wavy, curly, tightly curled.
Color: Black, brown, red, etc., note if dyed.
Hairline: Low on forehead, receding, "widow's peak" at center, etc.
Style: Neatly combed, unkempt, parted, short, long.

Eyebrows
Straight   Arched
Up Slant   Down Slant
Irregular   Irregular

Eye Shapes
Round   Oval
Up Slant   Down Slant
Wide Open   Close Lidded
Low Pupils   High Pupils
Large Pupils   Small Pupils

Nose
Shape: Long, wide, flat, pug, Roman, etc.

Cheeks
Flesh: Sunken, filled out, dried, oily.
Wrinkles: "Caliper" lines beside nose, mouth (if marked), other.

Cheek Bones
Prominence: High or low, wide or narrow, fleshy.

Forehead
Height: High, low, wide, narrow.
Skin: Smooth, light or heavy creases, wrinkled.

Ears
Size: Large, small, etc.
Prominence: Protruding or flat against head

Mouth
Corners: Turned up, turned down, level.
Upper Lip: Thin, medium, full.
Lower Lip: Thin, medium, full.

Chin
Shape: Round, oval, pointed, square.
Peculiarities: Small, double, dimpled, cleft.

Neck
Front: Double chin, protruding Adam's apple, etc.
Sides: Hanging jowls, etc.

5

Chart 9.6. Robbery Description Form (continued)

In Case Of Robbery *Notify police and fill in the blanks.*   **Common Weapon Types**

| SEX | | COMPLEXION | |
| GLASSES *(Color, Type)* | | LONG BARREL REVOLVER | SNUB NOSE REVOLVER |

AGE	
RACE		SCARS/MARKS	
HEIGHT		HAT *(Color, Type)*		LARGE AUTOMATIC	SMALL AUTOMATIC
WEIGHT		TIE *(Color, Type)*		Bolt-Action
HAIR		COAT *(Color, Type)*		Lever
			SAWED-OFF RIFLES
EYES		SHIRT *(Color, Type)*		Pump
MOUSTACHE, BEARD		PANTS *(Color, Type)*		Automatic
TATTOOS		SHOES *(Color, Type)*		Single Shot
			SAWED-OFF SHOTGUNS

Source: (1, 5, 10).

10
External Fraud and Forgery: Ever-Increasing Problems

Two Major Forms of External Crime

Restaurants can be victimized by two other major types of external crime which are increasing at an astonishing rate: fraud and forgery. Restaurateurs must alert their employees to this ever-present crime threat and train them to minimize these types of criminal acts.

Fraud is the "fraudulent conversion and obtaining of money or property by false pretenses. Included are bad checks and confidence games," (13) but not forgeries or counterfeiting. The U.S. Department of Justice regards forgery and counterfeiting as "allied" crimes. These crimes are, "All offenses dealing with the making, altering, uttering [circulating as if legal or genuine], or possessing, with intent to defraud, anything false in the semblance of that which is true." Included are:

- Altering or forging public and other records.

- Making, altering, forging, or counterfeiting bills, notes, drafts, tickets, checks, credit cards, etc.

- Forging wills, deeds, notes, bonds, seals, trademarks, etc.

- Counterfeiting coins, plates, banknotes, checks, etc.

- Possessing or using forged or counterfeited instruments.

- Erasures.

- Signing the name of another or fictitious person with intent to defraud.

- Using forged labels.

- Possession, manufacture, etc., of counterfeiting apparatus.

- Selling goods with altered, forged, or counterfeited trademarks.

- All attempts to commit the above. (13)

Credit Card Fraud and Forgery

There is no doubt that credit cards are an asset to businesses. They provide guests with a convenient method to pay for goods and services. Unfortunately, credit cards also represent a significant threat to profits for unwary business operators.

Losses from credit card fraud exceeded $200 million in 1982, a 300 percent increase from 1979. (3) By 1986, annual credit card fraud losses were estimated at $700 million.

Although credit card fraud is a federal offense, it is often assigned a lower priority than many other crimes because it is nonviolent. In recent years lobbying for stronger credit card fraud penalties has intensified. The Counterfeit Access Device and Computer Fraud and Abuse Act of 1984 was the "first significant federal effort to deal with the problem." (4) The law makes credit card fraud a felony with fines up to $50,000 (or twice the amount of the fraud) and prison terms of up to 15 years. The law also empowers the United States Secret Service to investigate credit card crimes. (4)

Since credit cards are an integral part of the restaurant business, it is essential that restaurateurs and their employees are aware of the types of credit card fraud and forgery that can occur in a restaurant, the facility's liability, and the precautions needed to prevent fraudulent use of credit cards.

There are three basic categories of credit card fraud:

- Use of an invalid card by the cardholder or unauthorized use of the card by a family member.

- Use or sale of an illegally obtained credit card or card number.

- Use of an altered or counterfeit card.

Cardholders may intentionally or unknowingly use invalid cards. The card may be cancelled, revoked, expired, or it may not be valid until a future date. In other cases, a member of the cardholder's family may use a nontransferable card or use the card without the cardholder's authorization.

Cards can be illegally obtained through robbery, burglary, or larceny, or they can be retained by a person to whom they were given for payment of goods or services. The person obtaining the card either personally uses the card or sells the card to another person.

Using counterfeited credit cards is the fastest growing type of credit card fraud. "Counterfeiting is growing because it's easier to steal an account number than an actual card—which is often reported missing soon after it's lost." (8) Counterfeit cards duplicate the credit card information of a valid account and can generally be successfully used by thieves to make purchases until the issuing company sends a bill containing the counterfeit card charges to an account's owner.

The information necessary to counterfeit a card—cardholder's name, account number, card expiration date, and other data—is obtained in various ways, such as:

- From a dishonest employee at a credit card company, banking institution, or any business that accepts credit cards. (3)

- By searching for credit card slip carbons through the trash barrels of establishments that accept credit cards.

- Through telemarketing schemes in which cardholders give account numbers to "phone callers posing as bank representatives or telephone canvassers. (One well-known scheme is to call cardholders, tell them that they have won a prize, and then request a credit card number as proof of identity.)" (11)

Controlling Credit Card Fraud and Forgery

As with any other crime, prevention is the most productive manner of dealing with credit card fraud and forgery. Credit card issuers use various techniques to make their cards difficult to duplicate. They now issue cards with three-dimensional designs, holograms, special magnetic tapes, ultraviolet inks, fine-line printing (rows of repeated symbols, words, or phrases), micro-printed bank identification numbers (BINs), and encoded (instead of embossed) account numbers.

Some credit card companies are experimenting with credit cards embedded with a computer chip that contains information about the account. Information can include "everything from a digital portrait of the card user's signature to a credit limit and record of the card's last 200 transactions. . . Before the merchant's terminal will approve a purchase, the . . . card user must type a code number, like the kind used in bank teller machines." (6)

The more sophisticated the prevention technology becomes, the harder it will be for counterfeiters to reproduce the original card. Since advanced security technologies are costly to implement, measures are somewhat slow in being introduced. However, the continued growth of credit card fraud and forgery is making these measures essential to reduce losses.

Preventing credit card fraud in a restaurant begins with verifying a credit transaction in accordance with the card issuer's procedures and keeping a record of such verification. When their procedures are not followed, or restaurants have no proof of adhering to such procedures, card companies do not have to reimburse a restaurant for its resulting losses. If a restaurant does not collect from the card company, it is unlikely that it will recover its losses even if the person who submitted the card is apprehended. Frequently, the legal costs of collection are greater than the amount lost through the fraudulent transaction.

Because the procedures stipulated by credit card issuers are so important, it is good practice to include them in policy and procedure manuals, teach them in employee training sessions, and have them available in writing for the employees who process them.

Typical credit card handling policies include:

- **Examine the card.** Watch for:

  "Altered, expired, or not-yet-valid credit cards." (1)

  Signatures on sales slips that do not match cards.

  "Cards that do not register imprints on carbon copies." (1)

- **Know the floor limit.** Most card issuers permit a floor limit, up to which a guest may charge without having a charge validated. Although the following precautions seem obvious, they are often overlooked in the press of time. A restaurant employee may accept a charge under the floor limit only if: (1)

The account number does not appear on the advisory sheet.

The guest's signatures match on card and charge slip.

The card has not expired.

- **Verify the account and its ownership.** According to a crime prevention expert, many operators mistakenly believe that they are protected when they call for an approval number for charges over the floor limit. Calling and receiving an approval code only indicates "that the given credit card number does exist, that it has a credit limit balance sufficient to cover the purchase, and that is has not been reported lost or stolen." (5) For this, as well as other reasons, some facilities request additional identification—such as a driver's license—to ensure that the person presenting the card is an authorized user.

The Council of Better Business Bureaus recommends that operators can further reduce chances of credit card fraud by: (1)

- Using electronic authorization terminals, calling credit card issuers for authorization on all credit card transactions, or conducting random authorization checks on small purchases.

- Requiring a valid photo identification for acceptance of credit card purchases.

- Copying the name, address, and telephone number of every credit card customer from the photo [or other] I.D., and then asking the authorization center to verify that information.

- Keeping a list of local bank telephone numbers near each cash register and checking local card BINs with the issuing bank. Calling telephone directory assistance after banking hours. Directory assistance will not provide addresses, but will verify given addresses.

- Checking carbon copies to be certain that clear imprints have been made. The carbon paper, which contains the imprint of the credit card number should be destroyed, or restaurants should use carbonless-type receipts or perforated carbons that split after use.

As an additional precaution, restaurant operators may wish to have external checks on their credit card handling procedures. To do this, they can have trusted individuals outside the restaurant, either acquaintances or professional service personnel, patronize the facility, pay with a credit card, monitor, and report on the techniques used by employees to check credit cards. Following the procedures listed above has two benefits: 1) fraudulent transactions can be identified before they are completed; and 2) the restaurant gains a reputation for thoroughness, making it an unlikely candidate for fraud.

Check Forgery and Fraud

Check fraud is so prevalent, that many businesses, including most restaurants, refuse to accept personal checks. However, some establishments, especially those that do not accept credit cards, will accept checks in accordance with strict procedures. An American Bankers Association representative stated that "One percent of all checks written each year, or about 400 million dollars, involve forgery." (7)

In the absence of security procedures, nearly any type of check—no matter what its origin—can be redeemed fraudulently. Types of checks include:

- **Personal checks.** These have been printed by a financial institution and are written and signed by the account holder.

- **Two-party checks.** A two-party check is "issued by one person to a second person who endorses it so that it may be cashed by a third person." (10) Types of two-party checks operators may be asked to cash include personal, payroll, or government checks. These checks can be used fraudulently because it is difficult to assess whether the second party (who is turning the check over to the restaurant) has a legal right to the check. Also, in some cases, the restaurant operator has no idea whether the originator of the check is creditworthy.

- **Blank checks.** These checks do not contain preprinted information. They can be purchased in stationery or other types of stores and filled out with the checkwriter's name, address, bank name, and account number.

- **Counter checks.** These are issued by a financial institution "to depositors when they are withdrawing funds from their accounts." (10) These checks are not negotiable—they can only be cashed at the issuing institution.

- **Traveler's checks.** These are "sold with a preprinted amount [to people] who do not want to carry large amounts of cash." (10) The checks are signed when they are purchased, and again when they are used to buy goods and services—so the signatures can be compared.

There are several types of fraudulent checks:

- **Checks drawn on closed accounts or accounts with insufficient funds.** The account holder knowingly writes a check without having the funds to cover it.

- **Falsified legitimate checks.** These are stolen checks which are forged or altered. "The amount of the legitimate check can be increased by altering a figure or adding a zero" (1).

- **Falsified checks on legitimate bank accounts.** "These include stolen blank checks and high-quality photocopies or other reproductions of legitimate blank checks." (1)

- **Completely falsified checks.** "The person passing the check may have fabricated or printed it and forged the signatures and endorsements. These checks are often drawn on bank accounts that are nonexistent or defunct—sometimes even the bank (or account owner) identified on the check is nonexistent." (1)

Check fraud usually goes undetected until the check is deposited and the bank reports that the check was drawn on insufficient funds, on a nonexisting account, or on a closed bank account.

Of the four types of bad checks, the predominant type restaurants have to contend with is the legitimate check written on an account with insufficient funds. This type is extremely bothersome and costly in terms of recovery procedures and labor expenses, but there is often a good chance of recovery. Usually, many bad checks received by restaurants are due to guests' carelessness or innocent mistakes. They are, however, bad checks and must be dealt with in order to recover the funds they represent.

Banks often run checks drawn on insufficient funds through the account a second time (unless bank fees are prohibitive) in case the guest simply made a timing error in depositing funds. If the check is returned a second time, restaurateurs usually attempt to collect by contacting the guest and requesting payment. Some restaurateurs prefer to send a letter or make a telephone call prior to sending a letter. They often deal directly with the guest to save the collection fee which would be charged if the problem was turned over to a collection agency or lawyer. Collection agencies are used when guests are uncooperative and if the amount of the bad check warrants the expense of a fee.

A special record should be maintained containing a list of bad-check incidents and names of persons who are poor credit risks. However, this list should *not* be tacked up in plain sight for all to see. The restaurant may not publicly display this information as it is considered an invasion of the privacy of those persons on the list.

Because checks drawn on insufficient funds can be innocent errors, some restaurateurs are lenient with first offenders and continue to extend them check payment privileges; others withhold future check-writing privileges from all offenders.

The passing of bad checks is a prevalent and costly crime. Employees must know proper check handling procedures and be alert to possible trouble spots when accepting checks. Effective check handling procedures begin with determining the types of checks that are accepted by the facility and the maximum amount of funds that are acceptable for each type. Restaurant policies must state which types of checks are not acceptable—frequently, facilities accept only personal checks for the amount of the customer's purchase and will not take foreign checks, checks from minors, checks on out-of-state banks, or second-party checks.

Next, with the needs of their clientele in mind, operators need to develop a check verification process. Local restaurants with many regular guests may have more lenient checkwriting policies than facilities with many transient guests. Chart 10.1 lists typical check handling procedures.

In many establishments, final check approval is the responsibility of the manager or other senior employee. It is critical that, although these employees are often dealing with a host of demands and are time-pressed, every check is examined to be sure all security procedures were properly followed.

Restaurateurs can obtain information on the many detection devices available from security device companies. If restaurateurs wish to install detection devices, they should know which ones will best meet their needs and be acceptable to their clientele.

In addition to developing procedures for handling check transactions, operators must be able to convey the message that the restaurant uses strong security measures. Many bad check passers will not try to defraud a facility if they perceive that security is tight.

The overall success or failure of check fraud and forgery precautions, however, will always rest with the personnel who receive checks from guests. Many frauds and forgeries are successful because the preventive techniques and detection methods available were not used.

Chart 10.1. Typical Employee Check Handling Procedures

- **Examine the check.** Make sure the check is fully and correctly filled out in nonerasable ink. Checks written in pencil or erasable ink can be easily altered.

  Watch checkwriters sign the checks. If in doubt about a signature, ask the customer to sign again and compare the signatures.

  Check the date, amount, "paid to" line, and signature. Make sure the facility's name is written correctly. Checks must have the current date.

  Check the row of digits at the lower left-hand corner of the check. The first two digits on the left can help verify the check. These two digits represent the Federal Reserve district number and give the state location of the issuing bank. The number must correspond to the bank address on the face of the check. Chart 10.2 lists the Federal Reserve code numbers.

  Be especially cautious in accepting out-of-area checks.

  Inspect traveler's checks as carefully as personal checks. Traveler's checks should be signed in the receiver's presence. If checks have been previously endorsed, ask the passer to re-sign the check and compare all three signatures. If endorsement does not closely match the authorized signature, the issuer can refuse to redeem the check.

  When suspicious, contact the bank the check is drawn on or use a verification service or system. If this is not possible, politely refuse to accept the check as payment.

  Remember any type of check can be fraudulent, or a guest can put a "stop payment" on it.

- **Require identification.** Ask guests to provide a minimum of two forms of identification. Driver's licenses and major credit cards are the preferred types, and are even more reliable when

Chart 10.1. Typical Employee Check Handling Procedures (continued)

they contain photographic identification. Social Security cards are usually not an acceptable form of identification, since these are easily obtained and cannot be used to trace the checkwriter.

Request additional information from people passing out-of-area checks. Ask for a local address and telephone number.

Never accept unfamiliar identification.

- **Examine identification.** As with checks themselves, identification may not be legitimate.

New identification cards may not be legitimate.

Be sure the physical description and/or photograph match the person.

When suspicious, check telephone numbers and addresses with telephone directories. As an added precaution, call the listed number for verification.

When possible, note vehicle license numbers on checks.

- **Use additional precautions.** Various types of checks require additional precautions.

If accepting a second-party check, do not cash these checks outside of business or banking hours without investigation.

Do not accept bank counter checks—these can be cashed only at the bank on which they are drawn.

Call the issuing bank to verify certified checks.

Use as much caution in accepting a cashier's check as is used when taking a personal check.

Inspect government checks carefully. "United States Treasury and state checks, for example, usually include the purpose of payment on the face, e.g., 'So. Sec.,' 'Ret.,' 'Tax Ref.,' 'CSF Annuity,' 'V.A. Ed.,' etc. Ask the person why the check was issued. The presenter should be able to tell you without hesitation." (16) If the person seems an unlikely recipient of the check based on the purpose noted on the check, be especially wary. The person could be attempting to pass a stolen check. An example of this would be if a juvenile was attempting to pass a retirement check.

Chart 10.1. Typical Employee Check Handling Procedures (continued)

Compare the endorsement on the check with other identification. If the check was preendorsed, have the passer reendorse it.

Do not accept checks signed with rubber stamps without knowing the maker and the payee.

- **Don't rush check verification procedures.** Do ask more questions when suspicious. People who pass bad checks prefer to work quickly. Never rush a transaction. Investigate each check that is presented. Employees should notify restaurant managers or owners if they become aware of fraud at any point during a transaction. The owner or manager can contact the police if necessary.

- **Initial the check.** Most facilities require employees to initial checks after completing transactions to indicate that they have followed all check-handling procedures.

Source: (1, 9, 16).

Chart 10.2. Federal Reserve Code Numbers

---

1   Connecticut, Maine, Massachusetts, New Hampshire, Rhode Island, Vermont
2   Connecticut, New Jersey, New York
3   Delaware, New Jersey, Pennsylvania
4   Kentucky, Ohio, Pennsylvania, West Virginia
5   District of Columbia, Maryland, North Carolina, South Carolina, Virginia, West Virginia
6   Alabama, Florida, Georgia, Louisiana, Mississippi, Tennessee
8   Arkansas, Illinois, Indiana, Kentucky, Mississippi, Missouri, Tennessee
9   Michigan, Minnesota, Montana, North Dakota, Wisconsin
10 Colorado, Iowa, Kansas, Missouri, Nebraska, New Mexico, Oklahoma, Wyoming
11 Arizona, Louisiana, New Mexico, Oklahoma, Texas
12 Alaska, Arizona, California, Hawaii, Idaho, Nevada, Oregon, Utah, Washington

---

Source: Food Marketing Institute (10).

Controlling Counterfeiting Losses

The United States Treasury Department reports that currency counterfeiting is again on the rise. (14) Despite this fact, counterfeiting currency is less common than credit card and check fraud or forgery. It is infinitely easier to produce a passable counterfeit credit card or check than to duplicate genuine currency. Also, it is easier to transport, pass, and profit from credit card and check fraud than from counterfeit currency.

As a threat to restaurateurs, counterfeit money is significant mostly because of the speed with which money changes hands under the pressure of doing business. Even poorly made counterfeits can slide by ordinarily vigilant employees who are in a hurry to go on to their next task.

Counterfeit money can be divided into two categories: expertly crafted reproductions, extremely difficult to detect, and amateurish attempts to reproduce the genuine article. Restaurant employees need special training to detect quality counterfeit money. However, even the untrained eye can detect amateurish counterfeits.

With the refinement of photo-offset printing processes, enterprising expert counterfeiters produce remarkably fine currency. However, this printing equipment is extremely expensive and is used only by a few. Even if such equipment is used, genuine currency has characteristics which are difficult to duplicate. It is made using fine inks and paper containing blue and red fibers. Because engraved plates are used to produce real currency, to the practiced eye it is always distinguishable from fake.

The United States Department of the Treasury offers the following information to help guard against counterfeit currency: "The United States uses the same paper in the manufacture of all its currency. There are three types of United States paper currency in circulation. The name of each type appears on the upper face of the bill. The different types of bills are further identified by the color of their Treasury seal and serial numbers." (14)

The three types of paper currency are: (15)

- **Federal Reserve Notes.** These have *green* serial numbers and a Treasury seal. Only $1, $5, $10, $20, $50, and $100 notes are currently printed. Chart 10.2 lists Federal Reserve code numbers, which identify the location of the Federal Reserve Bank that issued the note. These code numbers are found in each of the four quadrants on the face of the note.

- **United States Notes.** These bear *red* serial numbers and a Treasury seal. Only the $100 note is currently printed.

- **Silver Certificates.** These have *blue* serial numbers and a Treasury seal. Although they are no longer printed, a few are still in circulation.

Note: The $100 bill is the largest denomination now being printed.

The Treasury Department further advises that "one of the surest methods of recognizing a counterfeit note is to compare it with a genuine bill of the same denomination and series. Rubbing a bill will not prove whether it is genuine or counterfeit. Ink will rub off either type note. . . . This comparison can be further extended to the texture of the paper and the ink coloring. The counterfeit portrait is lifeless. Shading, such as in the head and hair and the cross-ruled lines behind the portrait, lacks sharpness and is often broken or missing." (15) Chart 10.3 compares features on genuine and counterfeit currency.

Another distinguishing factor in the detection of counterfeits is that district numbers (appearing in all four inside corners of the bill) must correspond to the Federal Reserve District letter inside the Federal Reserve seal. Chart 10.4 lists federal districts along with their corresponding number and letter. A list containing the district numbers and letter symbols should be on hand for all employees who handle money.

Using the information in the chart, an employee would check the paper currency to find the number in each inside corner, and would then check the list to see if the location matched the number. For instance, if the number, which appears four times, happened to be 6, then the letter inside the seal should be "F" to denote that the bill had been printed in Atlanta.

One common form of counterfeiting is called "Note Raising." This is accomplished by gluing counterfeit pieces, usually though not always corners, onto genuine bills of lesser denomination. It is wise for employees to familiarize themselves with all regular currency so that if, for instance, they were to see Alexander Hamilton's portrait on a bill that had "50" in every corner, they would be quick to detect the fraud. Chart 10.5 lists the correct illustrations for bill denominations.

The detection of counterfeit money, like the detection of credit card and check fraud or forgery, depends upon employee training and vigilance. The elements of haste and distraction work against vigilant

Chart 10.3. Comparison of Genuine and Counterfeit Currency

Feature	Genuine Currency	Counterfeit Currency
Portrait	Sharp, regularity of lines. Eyes are clear and distinct. Pronounced contrast and shading.	Flat, dull, smudgy. Background often merges into portrait. The lines are irregular and broken.
Treasury Seal	The saw tooth points around the rim are identical and sharp.	The saw tooth points may be uneven and broken.
Serial Numbers	Distinctive style, firmly and evenly printed. The same color as the Treasury seal.	May be a different printing style and poorly reproduced. Badly spaced or unevenly aligned.
Back of Note	Distinct and sharp details. The shading lines easily noticed.	Numerous green details and shading lines missing or merged into the solid green area.

Source: United States Department of the Treasury (15).

Chart 10.4. Federal Reserve Districts, Numbers, and Letters

District	Number	Letter
Boston, Massachusetts	1	A
New York, New York	2	B
Philadelphia, Pennsylvania	3	C
Cleveland, Ohio	4	D
Richmond, Virginia	5	E
Atlanta, Georgia	6	F
Chicago, Illinois	7	G
St. Louis, Missouri	8°	H
Minneapolis, Minnesota	9	I
Kansas City, Missouri	10	J
Dallas, Texas	11	K
San Francisco, California	12	L

Source: Oklahoma Retail Grocers Association (12).

Chart 10.5. Bill Denominations and Corresponding Illustrations

Bill Denomination	Portrait On Front	Illustration On Back
One	George Washington	U.S. Seal
Five	Abraham Lincoln	Lincoln Memorial
Ten	Alexander Hamilton	U.S. Treasury
Twenty	Andrew Jackson	White House
Fifty	Ulysses S. Grant	U.S. Capitol
One hundred	Benjamin Franklin	Independence Hall

Source: The Council of Better Business Bureaus (1).

---

efforts in these cases. In fact, counterfeiters may create a hurried or distracting situation in order to put employees off guard.

When Fraud Occurs

Despite the best preventive efforts, some fraud will occur. A restaurant can minimize its effect by knowing how to recover as much money as possible.

As mentioned earlier in the chapter, reimbursement by credit card issuing companies depends greatly upon a restaurant's ability to prove that employees followed stipulated verification procedures. When correct security measures have been followed, the issuing company usually reimburses the restaurant.

With fraudulent checks, responsibility for recovery of losses falls upon the restaurateur, who can follow the procedures detailed earlier in this chapter. In cases where a bank notifies the restaurant that a guest's check is fraudulent, the restaurant operator should immediately contact the police department. It is also a good idea to notify other branches of the restaurant, the local Chamber of Commerce, and any other agencies that can help prevent the fraud from happening at another business. If it is an out-of-state check that is bad, the FBI is notified because passing a bad out-of-state check is a federal offense. (1)

A returned check should be kept in a secure place, in a sealed envelope, without marking or stapling it. It should be handled as little as possible, and it should be retained as evidence should the check passer be apprehended. Prosecuting offenders is worth the effort. It is a deterrent to other bad check passers because they will get the word that the restaurant will be tough on them if they are caught.

Counterfeit money is the responsibility of (and constitutes a loss for) the person to whom it has been passed. Therefore, if detection methods fail, or if they succeed and a passer is identified, the police should be called immediately and the Secret Service (a branch of the United States Department of the Treasury) should be notified. Even if the person attempting to pass the counterfeit is known and trusted by the restaurateur, the counterfeit money should not be returned to that person. The money must be turned over to the authorities who will need to know the following: (15)

- From whom did the restaurant receive the bill?

- Was the counterfeit bill given in payment for merchandise or services?

- Is the identity of the passer known?

- Is the passer still present or in the immediate area?

- Are there accomplices in the area?

- Did the passer have the opportunity to discard other bills or evidence?

Facts gathered through such investigations are used by the authorities to apprehend and prosecute those involved.

To protect against credit card or check fraud or forgery, or counterfeit currency, restaurateurs must decide the lengths to which they are willing to go to reduce their losses. They must be aware of what they can do, and they must then decide to what degree they will go in terms of detection procedures.

Once these decisions have been reached, operators must establish, maintain, and monitor security systems. Employees should understand that following established security procedures is one of their job responsibilities and that they may be dismissed if they do not do so. With comprehensive and firm security checks in place against these external crimes, restaurateurs should be able to diminish the financial losses that would otherwise occur.

11
Other External Threats

Larceny-thefts: When Guests Are Involved

A restaurant's guests can be larceny-theft victims or perpetrators. "Larceny-theft is the unlawful taking, carrying, leading, or riding away of property from the possession of another. All thefts that are not part of a robbery, burglary, or motor vehicle theft [are] classified in this category regardless of the value of the article stolen." (21) Larceny-thefts include:

- Pocket picking.
- Purse snatching.
- Shoplifting.
- Thefts from motor vehicles.
- Thefts of motor vehicle parts and accessories.
- Thefts of bicycles.
- Thefts from buildings (where the offender has legal access).

- Thefts from coin-operated devices or machines.
- All other larceny not specifically classified.

Larceny-theft occurs in restaurants when a guest takes cash from a register drawer, a patron's wallet is stolen, personal belongings are taken from the facility's checkroom, or something is taken from a guest's automobile when it is parked in the restaurant's lot. (Theft of the automobile itself is categorized as motor vehicle theft, not larceny.)

Theft of Property

Because facing the reality of crime is unpleasant, many restaurateurs are tempted to ignore problems and regard the damage done by theft or other crimes as a cost of doing business. This laissez-faire attitude was discussed in Part I, but the attitude is perhaps even more pervasive when operators must deal with crimes committed by restaurant guests or suppliers.

The fact is, some guests and suppliers do commit larceny-theft. If restaurateurs ignore such acts, they actually foster an increase in such crimes. *Crime prevention begins with managers who convey the message that criminal acts will not be tolerated and criminals will be prosecuted.*

Larceny-theft of Guest Property

Restaurant service must extend to meeting guests' needs even when their property has been stolen. Although restaurants are not liable for unchecked stolen belongings, they must show the guests that the facility is concerned and will be as helpful as possible. When guests' property is stolen, employees should attempt to calm the guests and provide the necessary assistance such as calling the police. If wallets or pocketbooks are stolen, restaurant operators typically make arrangements for guests to pay for their meals at a later date.

Laws concerning operator liability for checked belongings vary by state. Facilities often post signs stating what types of belongings can be checked and describing the extent of their liability if an item is stolen. Many will not accept fur coats or other valuables or be responsible for exotic cars parked in their parking lots. Restaurant checkroom and parking attendants must be well-drilled regarding company procedures in how to handle guests and to contact managers when unfortunate incidents do occur.

When Guests Commit Larceny-theft

Sadly, not all restaurant guests are honest. They may steal from facilities in various ways. One of the most common forms of guest theft occurs when guests leave the facility without paying for their meals or deny the validity of credit card charges (this is often called "stiffing").

Stiffing problems can be solved in several ways. One method is to place the cash register near the exit so guests must pass the cash register in order to leave the facility. Cashiers should be positioned so they can observe guests at all times; they should not have to turn their backs on guests. When servers are responsible for collecting payment, they should be trained to notice when guests are preparing to leave, and should present guest checks promptly. Fast-service restaurants typically solve stiffing problems by requesting that patrons pay for their meals before the order is filled. When guests pay with credit cards, they should be asked to sign both guest checks and credit card slips.

Other guests may attempt to steal restaurant property including table appointments such as silverware, linens, peppermills, menus, ashtrays, rugs, and vases. "Size does not deter the restaurant thief . . . A 3- × 5-foot Oriental rug was rolled out of one restaurant a few years ago. Every summer, another restaurant loses about a half dozen chairs from its outdoor patio. And at a third restaurant, an 8-foot rubber plant disappeared shortly after the restaurant opened." (13) As one manager notes, "People will steal anything and everything they can get out the door." (13)

Theft of tableware can be discouraged if employees are attentive and remove soiled or unused items from the table as soon as possible. *Removing temptation is an effective method of theft prevention.* For example, some restaurants solve the problem of stolen peppermills by having the server grind the pepper for guests. Others completely remove the temptation by using less elaborate tableware. They use earthenware instead of bone china, glass instead of crystal goblets, and stainless rather than silverplated flatware. However, removing temptation is not always possible, especially in fine-dining establishments where lavish tableware contributes to their image.

Larceny-theft is not limited to the removal of property. Guests also steal by:

- **Claiming that valid credit card charges are fraudulent.** Some guests charge a meal, then refuse to pay the bill when it is sent by the charge card company. They may claim that the charges were unauthorized. To prevent losses from this type of theft, restaurants have guests sign both guest checks and credit card slips and retain both as proof the charges were incurred.

- **Altering a guest check and paying a lesser amount.** These losses can be avoided if guest checks are written in nonerasable ink or printed by electronic equipment. When a server or cashier has made an error on a check, it should be voided and rewritten rather than altered, and the guest should be asked to sign the new check. When guests have surreptitiously altered the figures on a guest check, they can be given a new check and told that the original check had been totaled incorrectly.

- **Deliberately failing to note arithmetic errors in their favor or omissions from the guest check.** This type of theft can be avoided if employees follow company procedures to ensure that checks are correct and always use electronic devices to total guest checks no matter how small the check.

- **Using a "quick change" routine.** A "quick change" transaction occurs when a patron pays the guest check with a bill of large denomination, receives the change from the cashier, "discovers" a smaller bill and asks to pay with the smaller bill without returning the change given on the larger bill. The cashier gives back the larger bill, takes the smaller bill, and gives the guest additional change. The guest "ends up walking away with all of the change from the smaller bill plus all or part of the change issued on the larger denomination." (5) When a "customer attempts to exchange a smaller bill for the original larger bill, the cashier should retrieve the change . . . return it to the cash register, [give the large bill back to the guest,] and start over with the new bill. Until the sale has been completed, the guest's and the cash register's money should not be mingled." (5)

- **Claiming insufficient change was given.** Claims of insufficient change can be avoided if employees leave the money given to them on the register or tip tray until the guest is satisfied with the accuracy of the transaction. (2) Some facilities find that electronic cash control systems are useful to combat this type of theft, as well as losses that occur when employees steal from the register. One company has introduced an electronic cash system that is attached to a safe. The cashier inserts money into a slot, and the correct change and a receipt are dispensed. (16)

Experienced restaurateurs have a variety of techniques for confronting guests who steal. Some operators believe that in the case of small thefts of property, an ashtray or a salt shaker, for example, it is best to give the guests an opportunity to put back the items they have taken. At one New York restaurant that has lost dozens of peppermills, servers have been trained to first look for the peppermill on the table and then ask the guest, "I'm looking for the peppermill, do you see it on the floor?" (9) Other operators present bills to guests for missing items. But to do so, they must be absolutely certain that the property has been stolen—that means that an employee must have seen the guest take and conceal the item or items.

Most facilities only permit the manager, owner, or security personnel to confront guests who have committed theft. These personnel must be tactful and avoid using words such as "thief," "crook," or "stolen." Nonaccusatory statements such as, "You're welcome to purchase the teapot," let guests know they have been caught. Confrontations must be discreet. Personnel may ask the guest to discuss the matter in a private area of the facility away from other guests. However, coercion cannot be used. If the suspect refuses to cooperate and move to another area, calling the police may be necessary.

If the suspect is willing to talk with the manager in a private office, the meeting should take place in an unlocked room. Suspects cannot be held against their will. If the customer is female, there should be a female employee present. These meetings must be brief.

When the cost of a stolen item is large enough to warrant prosecution, it is best to let the police handle the situation since there are many ways to inadvertently violate a suspect's rights. Restaurant employees must understand that although they are positive a guest is guilty of theft, they cannot violate the guest's rights in any way.

Vendors Who Steal

Theft resulting from collusion between vendors and employees was discussed in the internal theft section of this text, but some forms of vendor theft occur without the assistance of dishonest employees. Methods vendors use to steal include: (4)

- **Delivering lesser quality items than ordered.** The vendor may ship products that are lower in quality than ordered. In other cases:

The delivery person suggests the receiver "'bulk weigh' several different cuts of meat, knowing the most expensive meat is short and the least expensive is overweight." (4)

Cartons are packed with high quality products on top and poor quality on the bottom.

• **Delivering lesser quantities than ordered.** Dishonest suppliers accomplish this in various ways. They may simply deliver a smaller quantity and hope the receiver does not check the shipment or they may:

Contend that "the rest of the shipment will be sent in a few days," but the additional products are never delivered.

Disguise underweight shipments by adding ice or extra packing materials to cartons.

Deliver products in cartons with incorrectly marked weights or quantities, hoping that the cartons will not be weighed, nor the contents counted.

Be overly helpful. Delivery people may bring deliveries directly to kitchen and storage areas before cartons are weighed.

Bring the correct quantity into the facility, but then secretly remove products and reload them onto their truck. Drivers may place cartons back on the truck after they have been unloaded and counted by receivers. Then they may offer to take "empty" cartons with them, but the cartons are far from empty—they contain merchandise.

• **Charging more than the agreed-upon price.** Dishonest vendors may make a verbal agreement to deliver products at a "special price," but then charge a higher price when the products are delivered.

Vendor theft can be curtailed by using correct purchasing and receiving procedures. These include:

• **Dealing with reputable vendors.**

• **Using purchase orders and specifications.** Purchase orders state quantities desired. In addition, they typically detail the agreed-upon price for each product, payment terms, credit or return conditions, day and time of delivery, packaging method, and any other pertinent information.

Specifications or "specs" are descriptions of the products being ordered. Typically, specs "state in clear and simple terms the name of the product to be purchased and all its pertinent characteristics. These may include its size, shape, weight, color, texture, moisture content, density, smell, fat content (in the case of meat products), etc. Frequently, the size is described by what is called a *count*, as in the case of hamburgers (either 4 to the pound or 6 to the pound) and dill pickle spears (90 to 100 to a number 10 can) . . . [In addition, specs] give a complete and accurate description of the way the product is to be packaged." (8) Specifications can be developed for food, equipment, services, and supplies. An example of a purchase specification is given in Chart 11.1

When purchase orders and specs are used, vendors know exactly what the operator wishes to purchase, and misunderstandings are less likely to occur. Copies of purchase orders and specifications should be given to receivers so that deliveries can be compared to orders. The following procedures should be observed:

- **Not purchasing "off the truck."** Some drivers offer to sell operators products they did not order. The driver may say, "I have an extra 25 6-ounce steaks. I can sell them to you at a special price." The driver may have gotten these products by

---

Chart 11.1. Example of a Purchase Specification

Item:	**Tiny Shrimp**
Description:	Small, cleaned, deveined, fresh frozen Indian shrimp—200 to 300 count per pound. Product should be clean, deveined, and free of feelers, shells, and extraneous matter. The texture must be firm, and the color should be gray or pink.
Packaging:	Five-pound quantities in poly bags with no staples used in the outer cartons. Outer carton must pass 300-pound test and have wax coating on the exterior.
Special Labeling Instructions:	Labeling must be clear and legible, stating count and meeting all local, state, and federal regulations.
Special Instructions/ Requirements:	Data sheets for bacteria analysis must accompany shipment of each lot.

Source: Kelly (8).

---

delivering smaller quantities to other customers. Receivers should not accept products that were not listed on purchase orders.

- **Scheduling deliveries for nonbusy periods.** Checking deliveries is a time-consuming task that requires the full attention of the receiver. Drivers should not be allowed to make unannounced deliveries.

- **Keeping the receiving area secure at all times.** The receiving doors should only be unlocked when deliveries are being made.

- **Never leaving delivery personnel alone in any area of the facility.** Only authorized persons should be allowed in the receiving area.

- **Having a responsible employee check orders upon delivery.** Responsible receivers should check all deliveries. This includes counting all items and making sure that products are not dented, damaged, out-of-date, or otherwise unacceptable. Drivers should not be permitted to assist receivers in checking orders. Deliveries must be compared to purchase orders and specifications. Pertinent information, such as product counts and the temperature of perishables, is typically recorded on receiving forms. Any overages, shortages, damages, temperature problems, or discrepancies are noted and brought to the attention of appropriate personnel so that returns and credits can be arranged. Delivery invoices should be signed only after deliveries have been checked and approved.

- **Checking cartons and not allowing any merchandise to leave the facility without a receipt.** Check all cartons the driver takes back to the truck and make sure that credit slips or other appropriate forms accompany any merchandise that the driver takes. Break down and dispose of all empty cartons.

Vandalism

"Vandalism consists of the willful or malicious destruction, injury, disfigurement, or defacement, of any public or private property, real or personal, without consent of the owner or person having custody or control, by cutting, tearing, breaking, marking, painting, drawing, covering with filth, or any such means as specified by local law." (21) Breaking windows and writing graffiti on surfaces are two common forms of restaurant vandalism. Youngsters out for "a good time" and disgruntled employees or former employees are often responsible.

Vandalism can be deterred by using many of the physical security methods discussed earlier. Well-lighted exterior areas, frequent patrols, and alarm systems reduce the likelihood of vandalism. If the facility is vandalized, the police must be notified. Operators should work with the police to try to determine who is responsible for the attack, and if additional security methods can be used to prevent future incidents.

Even seemingly insignificant forms of vandalism, such as a single smashed window or broken gate, can have serious consequences because vandalism often makes the facility more vulnerable to other external threats such as burglary. Therefore, it is important that operators arrange for additional security coverage as well as attending to the needed repairs as soon as an act of vandalism is discovered.

Drunkenness, Disorderly Conduct, and Assault

Situations leading to these types of crimes are emotionally charged and pose a threat to everyone present in a facility. When employees or guests get out of hand, managers or other designated employees must know how to react to minimize the consequences. They need to understand when intervention either by themselves or by the police is required.

"Drunkenness includes all offenses of intoxication, with the exception of 'driving under the influence'." (21) Preventing employees or guests from becoming drunk and disorderly is the optimum security measure. Employees who show signs of alcoholic intake should be relieved of their job responsibilities for the day at once. (Some companies have the policy that any drinking by an employee is grounds for immediate dismissal.)

Bartenders and servers should receive liquor service training so they know how to spot potential alcoholic beverage abusers and tactfully refuse guest service when necessary. When people begin to act disorderly, it is important for employees to remain calm and attempt to talk with them or guide them to an area of the facility where they can do the least harm to people or property. Employees should call for security personnel assistance or the police before a situation becomes uncontrollable.

On occasion, an assault is committed in a restaurant. "Aggravated assault is an unlawful attack by one person upon another for the purpose of inflicting severe or aggravated bodily injury. This type of assault usually is accompanied by the use of a weapon or by means likely to produce death or great bodily harm. The category includes the commonly entitled offenses of assault with intent to kill or to murder; poisoning; assault with a dangerous weapon; maiming, mayhem, and assault with intent to maim or commit mayhem; assault with explosives; and all attempts to commit the foregoing offenses." (21) A simple assault differs from aggravated assault in that no weapon is used and it does not result in "serious or aggravated injury to the victim." (21)

Any type of assault must be reported to the police both to prevent further injury to the parties involved and to protect the restaurant from legal suits.

Arson

Arson refers to "any willful or malicious burning or attempts to burn, with or without intent to defraud." (21) Fires caused by arson can be incendiary or suspicious. " 'Incendiary fires' are fires in which legal decision or physical evidence indicates that the fire was 'deliberately set.' 'Suspicious fires' are fires in which circumstances indicate the possibility that a fire may have been deliberately set, multiple ignitions were found, or there were suspicious circumstances and no accidental or natural ignition factor could be found." (21)

The media picture of arson is of a crime committed in the middle of the night to collect insurance money, but arson is not restricted to this scenario. Disgruntled current or former employees and disturbed outsiders have committed arson both at night and during restaurants' operating hours, and have caused destruction and death.

A restaurant's fire plans must include the possibility of arson, in which the spread of smoke or flames can be amazingly rapid. Without all-encompassing fire plans the following may occur: (10)

- **There is a greater chance of injury or death.** Guests and employees may become trapped or injured while attempting to leave the facility.

- **Response from fire departments is hampered.** Nervous employees may give fire departments incorrect or incomplete information when reporting fires.

- **Fire extinguishers and other systems may be used incorrectly.** Untrained employees may use fire extinguishers incorrectly or may turn off sprinkler systems prematurely.

- **Monetary losses may be higher due to a lack of cash controls.** Employees may neglect to lock cash registers or secure funds in fireproof safes.

Employees need to distinguish between fires that are small enough to be put out with fire extinguishers and fires that require evacuating the facility and notifying the fire department. "Fire extinguishers are for very small fires and cannot be relied upon to put out blazes of any great size. The fire department should be called before the fire extinguisher proves to be inadequate." (1)

When fire extinguishers are used, it is important to know the type (or class) of the fire, since some fire extinguishers are not approved for use on all types of fires. "Using an extinguisher on a fire for which it is not intended will either not extinguish the fire or perhaps spread the fire, or be dangerous to the safety of the extinguisher operator" and other people in the facility. (10) The four classes of fires are listed in Chart 11.2.

Approved extinguishers correspond to the types of fires they can be used to put out. In other words, Class A extinguishers are used for Class A fires, and so forth. Classes of fire extinguishers appear in Chart 11.3. Chart 11.4 gives operating instructions for each type of extinguisher.

Fire extinguishers used in restaurants should be approved by Underwriter Laboratories and the National Fire Protection Association. In addition, fire extinguishers must meet the regulations of the Occupational Safety and Health Administration.

Larger fires require evacuation of the facility and the assistance of fire officials. Fire department personnel need to be familiar with the layout of the restaurant. They can be given tours and/or supplied with maps of the facility. In addition, fire officials can advise restaurateurs on placement of emergency exits, types and placement of sprinkler systems and fire extinguishers, and evacuation procedures.

Employees must be trained to follow established evacuation guidelines to lessen the chances of injury. Regularly conducted fire drills

Chart 11.2. Classes of Fires	
Class	**Description**
Class A	Fires in ordinary combustible materials (such as wood, cloth, paper, rubber, and many plastics) which require the heat-absorbing or cooling effects of water or water solutions, the coating effects of certain dry chemicals which retard combustion, or the interrupting of the combustion chain reaction by halogenated agents.
Class B	Fires in flammable or combustible liquids, flammable gases, greases, and similar materials, which must be put out by excluding air (oxygen), inhibiting the release of combustible vapors, or interrupting the combustion chain reaction.
Class C	Fires in live or energized electrical equipment. Safety to the extinguisher operator requires the use of electrically nonconductive extinguishing agents. When electrical equipment is de-energized, extinguishers for Class A or B fires may be used.
Class D	Fires in combustible metals (these do not occur in restaurants).

Source: Miller (10).

help employees learn how to evacuate the building in emergency situations.

Typically, employees have specific responsibilities when it is necessary to evacuate a restaurant. Designated employees are responsible for:

- **Reporting fires.** All necessary information, such as the full name and address of the facility and emergency telephone numbers, should be posted near every telephone.

- **Informing and assisting guests.** Guests must be calmly informed that it is necessary to leave the building. They should be told to take their personal belongings and proceed to a fire exit. Some guests, especially those who are older, disabled, or have small children, may need assistance.

- **Handling accidents and crises.** Company handbooks usually contain procedure sheets for handling common emergencies.

- **Securing funds and records.** When possible, all funds should be placed in fireproof safes. When monies must be left in cash registers, the designated employees should lock registers before

---

Chart 11.3. Classes of Fire Extinguishers

Class	Description
Class A	For use on Class A fires. These are water type extinguishers—including pressurized water, hand-pump, and loaded steam extinguishers; soda acid extinguishers (water solutions containing bicarbonate of soda and sulphuric acid); and gas cartridge extinguishers where carbon dioxide gas expels the water.
Class A:B	For use on Class A or B fires. This class includes certain foam extinguishers. Foam extinguishers usually contain a solution of aluminum sulfate and bicarbonate of soda.
Class B:C	For use on Class B or C fires. This class includes dry chemical and pressurized carbon dioxide extinguishers.
Class A:B:C	For use on Class A, B or C fires. "Extinguishers in this class are referred to as tri-class or multi-purpose extinguishers. Dry chemical extinguishers using ammonium phosphate and extinguishers using Bromotriflouromethane or Bromocholordiflouromethane (Halon) carry the ABC rating." (10)

Source: (1, 10).

Chart 11.4. Operating Instructions for Fire Extinguishers

Type of Extinguisher	Operating Instructions
Foam	Do not direct the foam directly into the fire, the foam should fall lightly on flames.
Carbon Dioxide	Directly discharge as close to the fire as possible; first at flame edges, then gradually forward and upward.
Soda Acid/Gas Cartridge	Direct stream at base of fire.
Pump Tank	Place foot on footrest and direct stream at base of flames.
Dry Chemical	Direct at the base of the flames. In case of Class A fires, follow up by directing the dry chemicals at the material that is still burning.

Source: Educational Foundation of the National Restaurant Association (formerly NIFI)/Applied Foodservice Sanitation (1).

---

evacuating the building. Important records are secured in fire-proof safes or are removed from the restaurant.

- **Shutting off equipment.** HVAC equipment, gas valves, and other equipment are typically shut off.

- **Making statements to the media.** Only trained persons should be allowed to talk to media representatives. Employees should never make accusations or give names of people who may have been responsible for incendiary or suspicious fires.

- **Contacting the insurance company and other necessary individuals.** Typically, company headquarters, facility owners or managers, and the insurance company require a full report on the fire, including what was lost or damaged, and if any injuries were sustained.

- **Protecting the facility after the fire.** Facilities are vulnerable to burglary after fires. Protection services are often necessary.

Other External Crimes

The previously discussed external crimes are the most common ones facing a restaurant, but facilities are somewhat vulnerable to other crimes as well. These include: extortion in conjunction with food tampering, bomb threats, kidnapping, or other acts; terrorism; and murder.

Although most restaurants never have to deal with these crimes, they must be prepared for them in the event they do occur. Since employees are unlikely to have had experience dealing with these crimes, the restaurant's policies and procedures are their only guidelines for action that can help safeguard employees, families of employees, or guests.

Tampering, Bomb Threats, and Other Extortion-related Crimes

Although food tampering, bomb threats, or other forms of extortion are rare, they do happen. Tampering and bomb threats may come from various sources including disgruntled or former employees, extortionists, emotionally disturbed persons, or publicity-seeking terrorist groups. In addition to the immediate problems that arise when threats occur, facilities sometimes lose business because the publicity surrounding the threat frightens potential patrons.

Some in the food industry are especially concerned about tampering threats. They feel that as tamper-resistant packaging for over-the-counter medications becomes more sophisticated, tampering of the food supply will increase. As one industry expert said, "Given the tamper-resistant packaging required on nonprescription medicines nowadays, it requires extreme patience, cunning, and possibly even special equipment to poison an over-the-counter drug. But it would take little if any expertise to tamper with a ketchup bottle in a restaurant or contaminate a fast-service salad bar." (14) Others feel that the food supply is fairly safe, "Because people like to smell, touch and savor it, they are more likely to detect contamination." (17)

Most threats are hoaxes, but *every threat must be taken seriously.* Most threats are made in telephone calls, but some are contained in letters. Employees who answer telephones must know how to handle threatening calls. One industry expert suggests that operators, "Instruct all personnel who might answer the . . . telephone to take every threatening call seriously; don't hang up on the caller, get as much information as possible, listen for background noises and speech characteristics, dialects, slang, etc." (11) A call can then be evaluated as follows: (19)

- **Unspecific threats are usually hoaxes.** For example, if the caller says, "I'm going to destroy your restaurant" it probably indicates a hoax. When the caller is serious, the information is usually specific: "There's a bomb in your facility set to go off at 8:30 this evening unless you follow my instructions."

- **When threatening telephone calls are received, the employee needs to study the caller's voice.** "A caller who sounds like a juvenile or who is excited, talks rapidly, or in a jovial manner is probably making a hoax call. However, a caller who is deliberate in speech, states a certain area where a bomb is placed, and/or gives a reason for placing the bomb, should be taken seriously." (19) In the case of a real threat, the caller will repeat the information to make sure that the person who answered the telephone understands the instructions.

The police must be notified immediately after threats are received. Bomb threats should be reported to the bomb squad, and tampering threats to the Federal Bureau of Investigation (FBI). Policies and procedures specifying whether searches are made or if the facility is to be evacuated vary. Some operators organize employees and begin searching for evidence following every threat, while others do nothing until the authorities arrive. When employees are responsible for conducting searches it is especially important to be discreet and thorough so as not to alarm guests and other employees. Typically, searches are conducted as follows: (11, 17, 19)

- **Designated employees are instructed to meet in a non-guest area.** Each employee is informed of the situation and assigned an area to search.

- **In the case of bomb threats, employees are instructed to look for suspicious packages or explosive devices.** When searches for evidence of tampering are being conducted, employees should look for "syringes, razor blades, pins, broken glass, pills, capsules, unidentified powdery substances," (11) and so forth. When tampering threats specify which foods are tainted, careful inspection is necessary. Some forms of tampering are easy to detect—a strong sweet almondy smell may indicate cyanide contamination (17)—but many tainted foods can smell and appear normal.

Facilities are usually evacuated when a bomb, suspicious package, or evidence of tampering is found. Evacuation procedures are the same as those for fires. In addition, the area surrounding a bomb or suspicious package must be secured. Procedures for securing these include: (19)

- Clear the area of all persons.

- Keep electrical units in the same operating position—lights and appliances that are on should remain on; those that are off should remain off.

- "Do not use walkie-talkie radios, or UHF or VHF portable radios within 300 feet of the device or package." (19) Citizens band (CB) radios should also not be used.

- Ask people wearing telephone beepers to shut them off.

Publicity surrounding threats and the way the threats are handled have an enormous impact on a restaurant's business. As with other crises, only company-designated employees should make statements to the media. While some operators feel that the business will suffer losses by informing the public of incidents, others feel that the public will feel more secure when they know a facility can effectively handle threats. This was the case when a Georgia chain received a tampering threat from an extortionist. By working closely with the FBI and then providing the public with a detailed account when the extortionist was arrested, the chain did not lose guests. According to a spokesperson, "We were flooded with letters of support from people all over the area." (15)

Although manslaughter (a person is killed by the gross negligence of another) or murder (a person is willfully killed by another) are heinous crimes restaurants are unlikely to have to deal with, there have been incidents in the past few years. Since these crimes always involve the police, a designated employee of the restaurant should be trained in techniques to facilitate a police investigation, and there should always be a restaurant spokesperson on hand to answer questions posed by the press.

These crimes are always in the public eye, and how a restaurant conducts itself will determine whether its image has been enhanced or its reputation suffers.

In Case of Emergency

The speed with which restaurant employees respond to emergencies caused by either accidental or criminal acts helps minimize injury and can even save lives. Next to every telephone in a restaurant there should be a list of the telephone numbers of people who provide emergency assistance. Chart 11.5 lists possible contacts to include. In addition, there should be at least one employee on the premises during all operating hours who has first-aid training. All necessary first-aid supplies should be on hand in a first-aid kit. "Some states have laws specifying the supplies that must be included in this kit; in general the kit will contain individually-wrapped sterile dressings, adhesive tape, slings, inflatable splints, and soap." (1)

When people suffer injuries, employees must know what they should or should not do to be of assistance. Chart 11.6 describes typical procedures for restaurant personnel to follow when people are injured in the restaurant.

Criminal acts and emergencies in any restaurant are stressful events with the potential to cause harm to people, property, and the restaurant's image. The negative effects of these acts are curtailed with the help of well-designed policies and procedures and employees who understand how to carry them out.

Chart 11.5. Emergency Telephone Numbers

Hospital
Ambulance service
First-aid squad / paramedics
Manager's home telephone
Owner's home telephone
Local police
State police
Fire department
Doctor
Dentist
Department of Health
Exterminator
Electric company
Gas company
Water company
Lawyer
Insurance agent
Auto towing and emergency repair
Local taxi
Equipment repair:
    Plumber
    Electrician
    Cooking equipment
    Refrigerator and freezer
    Ware-washing equipment
    Air conditioning
    Heating
    Other

Chart 11.6. Typical Procedures for Handling Injuries

- Call for emergency assistance immediately: an ambulance, a first-aid attendant, a paramedic, or a doctor.
- Do not move the injured person; do not help someone stand up, particularly if the person is bleeding or seems dizzy, confused, or in great pain.
- Provide only emergency first aid, following established medical procedures, in a serious or life-threatening situation.
- Do not administer drugs or treatments of any kind, not even "home remedies" such as aspirin, cold compresses, or a bandage for a sprain.
- Do not make statements about company insurance coverage or damage recovery policies to anyone.

12

What's Ahead?

The Need to Adapt

Security procedures in restaurants require continual change to keep up with the adaptability of dishonest people. As soon as one door is closed to internal or external crimes, the ingenuity of dishonest people will find new doors to open.

Innovations in computerized security controls are making many areas in restaurants less susceptible to theft. However, the same innovations are creating a new and potentially more sensitive area of activity—computer fraud. Restaurant firms will have to be increasingly alert to security precautions taken in protecting their computer record storage areas. The kind of thieves who will manipulate records and computer materials will very likely be better educated, at least in computer use, than the classic pilferer. For this reason, they may very well be more difficult to detect and apprehend.

According to the Council of Better Business Bureaus' handbook, *How to Protect Your*

Business, most computer crimes fall into one of five categories: (1)

1) *Programming activities.* An example would be a dishonest employee who programs a computer to issue payroll checks to fictitious employees. "Small companies, in which one employee often has sole responsibility for running the computer, are most vulnerable to this type of fraud." (1)

2) *Computer time.* The unauthorized use of an employer's computer facilities, whether for playing games or personal business "is perhaps the most costly and pervasive computer crime." (1)

3) *Input data.* "Tampering with data can include the addition of names of fictitious suppliers to lists of approved vendors. Subsequent instructions might then authorize payments ostensibly made to the nonexistent suppliers that actually find their way into the programmer's pockets." (1) Here, too, small companies are the most vulnerable.

4) *Output data.* This includes the theft of printouts or punch cards of mailing lists, guest lists, and copyrighted, patented, or other confidential information.

5) *Data transfer.* For example, an employee may use the computer to transfer funds to a personal account.

Security Precautions

Computer fraud in a restaurant is most likely to take place in the central computer control area and consist of altering records. This is a process that can be made very difficult by adequate record storage procedures. Copies of all storage media (disks, tapes, etc.) should be placed where they cannot be accessed by those who originally input the information. They should be reviewed by people other than those who did the inputing to monitor the transactions.

Recent studies have shown that it is not necessary to use high-tech tactics in most computer fraud. It is because of security weaknesses that most computer fraud succeeds.

The installation and monitoring of security measures for computer controls is a highly refined procedure. According to the *National Res-*

taurant Association News (now *Restaurants USA*), the following steps are critical to protect against computer fraud: (2)

- Limit physical access to vital areas to authorized personnel; eliminate nonessential doors; escort visitors at all times; involve all department personnel in access control; and make spot inspections to discourage removal of resources without written authorization.

- Make the computer department independent of all departments for which it processes information; segregate duties within the department so no one can commit fraud alone; and rotate duties on a random basis.

- Separate the computer records library from other computer functions and implement strict physical access and inventory controls; store critical data in locked vaults or safes; erase confidential information on tapes and disks before sending them out for recertification and cleaning; conduct regular and surprise inspections; and document library procedures.

- Make sure that console logs provide a printed record of all jobs processed, all operator activities, and anything done to the system. Logs should be reviewed by supervisory or managerial personnel at the end of each shift or once a day.

- Account for use of all input and output media—floppy disks, punched cards, paper tape, blank output forms, and so forth.

- Make password security strict and unbending. Longer passwords are safer but should be changed fairly often; nevertheless, all access attempts that are denied should log the pertinent information and introduce a ten-second delay.

- Observe backup and recovery procedures. Backup is critical to protect data from malicious or accidental destruction.

Refinements of fraud-proofing the computer installation will depend greatly on the type of computer system used. It is imperative that managers take a close look at how secure they have made their computer operation.

Whether computerized or not, the most sophisticated, foolproof security system in the world cannot guarantee 100 percent success. The best it can do is minimize theft by implementing effective controls, which will reduce the likelihood of theft by removing as much temptation as possible.

Probably the most important elements in a healthy security climate are the personal interactions among employees and between managers and employees. Much of the quality of behavior and trustworthiness of a restaurant's staff is due directly to the quality of relationships among managers and their employees. Managers must be properly trained in communication and in control procedures so that the problem of all types of theft decreases in the future.

Glossary

Accountability:
An essential ingredient of cash register control which makes employees responsible for cash register shortages. Accountability discourages theft and allows management to pinpoint problem sources.

Anti-theft Policy:
Restaurant regulations pertaining to the handling of money, food, and other property which employees are required to follow to discourage theft.

Automatic Liquor Dispensing System:
An electronic device that dispenses predetermined quantities of liquor and records the price of each drink. It is used as a component of internal beverage control.

Background Check:
Preemployment screening of a job applicant in order to determine honesty or suitability for employment.

Bank of Cash:
The amount of money assigned to each cashier at the beginning of each shift.

Body Language:
Nonverbal communication (involving postures, gestures, and facial expressions) which gives clues to a person's character.

Bonding Company:
A certified organization that investigates an employee's background for arrests and other indications of dishonesty. The bonding company will replace any money stolen on the job by a bonded employee.

Burglary:
The attempt to illegally get into a building, leaving evidence that force was used, or actually entering a facility with or without using force.

Cash Room:
An area of the restaurant where receipts are brought for accounting and safekeeping purposes.

Check Fraud:
Offering payment for goods or services with stolen checks, forged checks, falsified checks, and checks drawn on accounts with insufficient funds to cover them.

Code Card:
A custom-designed card made to fit into a slot which activates an electronic lock.

Combination Locks:
Locks which can be opened by dialing a specified series of numbers in specified directions (either left or right).

Computer Fraud:
The unauthorized use of a computer and/or the manipulation of automated control systems for the purpose of defrauding.

Console Log:
A computer record which shows the various jobs processed by a computer at any given time.

Conviction:
Being found guilty in a court of law of committing an illegal act.

Council of Better Business Bureaus:
A professional organization whose purpose is to promote fair business practices and help protect consumers.

Counterfeit:
Illegal production of imitation money or other legal tender for the purpose of fraud.

"Cover" Job:
A temporary position assigned to an undercover agent/detective for the purpose of gaining inside information in order to expose theft and/or other irregularities perpetrated by an employee or a group of employees.

Credit Bureau:
A company that investigates individuals or groups, maintains information pertaining to credit ratings, and issues credit reports.

Credit Report:
A written statement that provides information on whether or not a person or group is creditworthy.

Critical Data:
Sensitive computer records which should be kept under strict security.

Cross Checks:
A method of monitoring merchandise in a restaurant, from purchasing through distribution, as a means to deter theft.

Detail Tapes:
Printed cash register tapes which record transactions.

Disc Tumbler Locks:
Key activated locks usually used on automobiles, vending machines, desks, and cabinets. They offer limited protection due to their construction.

Electronic Locks:
Locks which are activated by code cards inserted into slots or by pushing buttons on their surface.

Embezzlement:
Internal crime involving fraudulent manipulation of cash, merchandise, or property for the purpose of theft. It is usually committed by highly placed personnel in positions of trust.

Entrance and Exit Control:
Specific doors (designated by management) which employees must use to enter and exit a facility. It is a component of internal control.

Federal Bureau of Investigation (FBI):
A branch of the United States Department of Justice. The FBI investigates crimes violating Federal laws (except those involving currency, tax, and postal laws) and brings the perpetrators of these crimes to trial.

Federal Reserve Code:
The first two digits in the lower left-hand corner of a check. These two numbers indicate the Federal Reserve District of the issuing bank, and can be used to verify a check's authenticity.

Forgery:
Defrauding or attempting to defraud by copying, changing, or otherwise falsifying legal tender or documents.

Fraud:
Passing bad checks, using confidence games, or falsifying information to unlawfully get possession of money or property belonging to another.

Garnishee:
A creditor may require an employer to withhold money from an employee's wages to satisfy a debt. Title I of the Federal Consumer Credit Protection Act stipulates that only a portion (usually 25% of the weekly take-home pay) of an employee's pay can be garnisheed.

An employer is also prohibited from firing an employee because wages have been garnisheed for any one indebtedness (for several garnishments based on different debts, it's another story).

High-risk Candidates:
Job applicants whose preemployment interviews and/or screening reveal emotional problems or character flaws (gambling, alcoholism, and so forth) that might lead to deviant behavior or dishonesty.

High-risk Employees:
Personnel with clean working records who might be tempted to steal due to occurrence of personal pressures or the onset of emotional problems.

Hologram:
Laser-printed 3-D images which are difficult to alter. Holograms are used on some credit cards to prevent credit card tampering.

Input/Output Media:
Computer supplies, such as floppy disks, punch cards, and forms used to hold information.

Integrity Shoppers:
People, unknown to a facility's employees, who are employed by management to periodically eat in the facility and report on all aspects of their dining experience. Sometimes, they test employee honesty.

Internal Accounting Controls:
Management-instituted checking of every control procedure pertaining to ordering, receiving, cash and check handling, bank statements, mail, bookkeeper duties, and all other internal accounting functions where theft might occur.

Internal Crime:
Illegal acts against the facility which are committed by its employees.

Internal Security:
Guidelines and procedures instituted by management to prevent theft.

Key Control:
Procedures devised by management to monitor keys as a means of preventing loss, tampering, and key duplication. It is a component of internal control.

"Lapping Sales":
A form of embezzlement usually involving small amounts of cash. If two identical checks are presented for payment, only one of the payments is rung on the cash register. The cash presented for the second check is pocketed. This type of skimming of funds can run into thousands of dollars if undiscovered.

Larceny-theft:
The stealing of cash or property from an individual or organization which does not include forcible entry into a property, the use of a weapon, or the threat of bodily harm.

Magnetic Locks:
A lock in which the tumblers consist of a series of magnets which are activated by a cylindrical key containing magnets.

Misconduct:
Illegal actions by employees that are costly to a restaurant, including sick leave abuse, falsifying time sheets, and on the job alcohol/drug abuse.

Multiple-line Cash Registers:
A system usually used in fast-service establishments where three or more cashiers are on duty at the same time making it difficult to keep track of which cashier has used which register during a shift of duty. Using this system, cashier accountability is very important to help prevent theft.

National Institute of Justice (NIJ):
A research branch of the United States Department of Justice.

Password Security:
Word or letter signals used to ensure that only authorized personnel have access to computer information.

Pin Tumbler Locks:
Key-operated locks which are fairly secure (plugs, cams, and pins are used in their construction) if they contain five or more pins.

Polygraph Test:
A test given to determine the honesty of an employee or job applicant. The physical reactions (such as blood pressure) that occur when a candidate answers questions are recorded on a polygraph machine. A polygraph test must be administered by an expert for reliable results.

Preemployment Screening:
Checking the background of job applicants as thoroughly as possible to ascertain whether they are honest and suitable for employment.

Preprogrammed Liquor Control Register:
A register that automatically records the price of a drink as it is dispensed.

Reflective Interviewing:
Responding to verbal communication or an employee complaint in a neutral and noncommittal style in order to indicate interest and understanding without being judgmental.

Robbery:
Unlawfully taking or attempting to take cash or property from a victim, using any type of weapon and/or using the threat of bodily harm.

Security Policy:
Rules, regulations, and methods of operation instituted by a restaurant to create a working environment that discourages employee dishonesty. This includes a code of ethics, inventory controls, and other systems of checks and balances.

Stock Card:
A written record kept in stock rooms that shows what merchandise has been removed and the date it was taken. It can be used to indicate what inventory should be in stockrooms at all times.

Strong-arm Tactics:
Forcibly taking cash or property from a victim, using only bodily force (fists, hands, or feet) as a weapon.

Tally Sheet:
A written record cashiers hand in to management which shows the amount of money in the register prior to and after their shift.

Telemarketing Scheme:
A form of credit card fraud using telephone scams. The object is to obtain a person's credit card number.

Theft:
See: *Larceny / theft*

Undercover Agents / Detectives:
Trained security personnel (either from inside an organization or hired from the outside) who work in areas where theft is occurring in order to obtain evidence and/or discover the sources of theft.

Vendor Collusion:

A form of theft in which employees work with an outside vendor to steal from the restaurant.

Vulnerable Area:

An area that is a tempting theft target because it contains valuables. In a restaurant, these include the cash register area, storage rooms, and cash rooms.

Wafer Tumbler Locks:

Disc tumbler, key-operated locks which are mainly used to ensure privacy, since they can easily be jimmied or picked.

References

OVERVIEW

Newspapers and Magazines

Foodservice Marketing

1. June, 1981
   "Security: How You Can Control Employee Theft"
   Frederick H. Rice

National Restaurant Association News

2. August, 1984
   "Tightening the Screws on Internal Security"
   Kathy Boyle

Nation's Restaurant News

3. October 22, 1984
   "Managing Human Resources—Staff Tries to Beat the System"
   Atid Kaplan

Occupational Hazards

4. June, 1984
   "Justice Department Study Puts Employee Theft Under the
   Microscope"

Other Publications

**United States Department of Justice—National Institute of
Justice**

5. "Theft By Employees in Work Organizations—Executive
   Summary"
   John P. Clark and Richard C. Hollinger
   September, 1983

CHAPTER 1

Books

1. Interviewing: Key to Effective Management
   Joseph P. Zimma
   GMI Engineering Management Institute
   Science Research Associates, Inc.
   Chicago, 1983

Newspapers and Magazines

Editor & Publisher

2. November 8, 1986
   "Employee Testing: A Hot Issue"
   Debra Gersh

National Restaurant Association News

3. August, 1984
   "Practical Suggestions for Tighter Security"
   William P. Fisher

Personnel Journal

4. August, 1986
   "The Work Environment—A Positive Guide to Theft Deterrence"
   Robert R. Taylor

Progressive Grocer

5. September, 1986
   "Honesty Tests: The Best Policy For Supers?"
   Robert Messina

Restaurant Business

6. October 10, 1986
   "Washington Watch—Polygraph Tests Now an Issue"
   Edmund Andrews

Restaurants & Institutions

7. October 1, 1986
   "NRA Opposes Banning Polygraph"
   Jeff Weinstein

8. May 13, 1987
"Polygraph Ban Gaining Support"
Robert Keane

Stores

9. June, 1986
"Loss Prevention Matters—Employee Theft"
Jules Abend

Other Publications

Money Management Institute

10. "Managing Your Credit," 1978

The Stanton Corporation

11. "The Stanton Survey," 1985

United States Department of Justice—Bureau of Justice Statistics

12. "Crime and Justice Facts, 1985," May, 1986

CHAPTER 2

Books

1. Food Store Security
Edited by Len Daykin
Progressive Grocer Co., New York, 1981

Newspapers and Magazines

Foodservice Marketing

2. June, 1981
"Security: How You Can Control Employee Theft"
Fredrick H. Rice

Personnel Journal

3. August, 1986
"The Work Environment: A Positive Guide to Theft Deterrence"
Robert R. Taylor

Security World

4. October, 1980
   "Employee Theft: The Reason Why"
   Donald R. Cressey
5. April, 1984
   "Employee Theft: A Costly Fringe Benefit"
   Kerrigan Lydon

Other Publications

Fair Oaks Hospital, Summit, New Jersey

6. "Role of the Supervisor—Warning Signs of Drug and Alcohol Dependency"

Loss Prevention Systems, Inc.

7. "In-store Security: Employee Theft"
   Written and presented by Charles I. Miller
   NOPA Retail Branch Stores Forum
   1985 Mid-winter Conference, Scottsdale, Arizona

SAGA

8. Loss Prevention Handbook

United States Department of Justice—National Institute of Justice

9. "Executive Summary: Theft by Employees in Work Organizations—A Preliminary Final Report"
   John P. Clark, Richard C. Hollinger, and Leonard F. Smith, with Phillip W. Cooper, Peter F. Parilla, and Philip Smith-Cunnien
   Research on Organizations and Occupations, Department of Sociology, University of Minnesota
10. "Theft by Employees in Work Organizations: Executive Summary"
    John P. Clark and Richard C. Hollinger
    September, 1983

CHAPTER 3

Books

1. Bar and Beverage Management
   David K. Hayes Ph.D. and Jack D. Ninemeier (consulting authors)
   Published for the Cornell University Home Study Program
   Foodservice Management Series
   Chain Store Publishing Company, 1987
2. How To Protect Your Business
   The Council of Better Business Bureaus
   The Benjamin Book Company in association with Prentice-Hall,
   Inc., 1985

Newspapers and Magazines

American Druggist

3. March, 1982
   "One Internal Theft Equals 40–50 Shoplifting Incidents"

Nation's Restaurant News—Restaurant Technology

4. July 2, 1984
   "Regulating the Usage of Manpower"
   Charles Forman

Other Publications

Small Business Administration

5. "Preventing Employee Pilferage"
   Saul D. Astor
   Management Safeguards, Inc.
   January, 1977

United States Department of Justice—National Institute of Justice

6. "Theft by Employees in Work Organizations: Executive Summary"
   John P. Clark and Richard C. Hollinger
   September, 1983

CHAPTER 6

Books

1. Food and Beverage Security: A Manual For Restaurants, Hotels, and Clubs
   Jack D. Ninemeier
   Boston: CBI Publishing Company, Inc., 1982
2. Psychology and Industry
   Norman R. Maier
   Boston: Houghton Mifflin & Co., 1955

Other Publications

Fair Oaks Hospital, Summit, New Jersey

3. "Role of the Supervisor—Warning Signs of Drug and Alcohol Dependency"

CHAPTER 9

Books

1. Food Store Security
   Edited by Len Daykin
   Progressive Grocer Co., New York, 1981
2. Management of Hospitality Operations
   Bruce H. Axler
   The Bobbs-Merrill Company, Inc., 1976

Newspapers and Magazines

The Chuck Wagon

3. March, 1981
   "Crime in the Restaurant"
   T. Nolin

Foodservice Marketing

4. June, 1981
   "Security: How You Can Reduce the Risk of Crime in Your Restaurant"
   Frederick H. Rice

Grocery Marketing (previously called Grocer's Spotlight)

5. January, 1984
"It's a Holdup! What Should You Be Doing? Experts Give Advice"
William F. Murphy

Progressive Grocer

6. October, 1985
"Violent Crime: Dealing with a Deadly Issue"
Michael Sansolo

Restaurants & Institutions

7. February 5, 1986
"Security Update"
Maureen Pratcher

The Wall Street Journal

8. November 8, 1984
"Security Drive: Fast-food Chains Act to Hold Down Crime and
Prevent Lawsuits—Hours and Sites Make Outlets Vulnerable to
Robberies; Those Harmed Often Sued—Greetings and Locked
Doors"
Elaine Johnson

Other Publications

Federal Bureau of Investigation

9. "Crime in the United States"
Uniform Crime Reports for the United States, 1985

Food Marketing Institute

10. "Food Marketing Institute Supermarket Security Manual"
Produced in Cooperation with Miller Brewing Company
Researched and written by Charles I. Miller, 1985

Law Enforcement Assistance Administration

11. "Commercial Security"
United States Government Printing Office, 0-237-092, 1977

SAGA

12. "Loss Prevention Handbook"

United States Department of Justice

13. "Sourcebook of Criminal Justice Statistics—1985"
Timothy J. Flanagan and Edmund F. McGarrell, Editors
Bureau of Justice Statistics
Washington, D.C.: United States Government Printing Office, 1986

CHAPTER 10

Books

1. How To Protect Your Business
The Council of Better Business Bureaus
The Benjamin Book Company in association with Prentice-Hall, Inc., 1985

Newspapers and Magazines

Consumer Views

2. April, 1986, Volume 17, Number 4
"Check or Card Fraud: Don't Let It Happen to You"

Forbes

3. September 9, 1985
"How the Smart Crooks Use Plastic"
John Merwin

The Journal of Commerce

4. December 31, 1984
"Credit Card Fraud Proliferates"
Martin Connolly

National Restaurant Association News

5. August, 1984
"Tightening the Screws On Internal Security"
Kathy Boyle

The New York Times

6. April 18, 1985
   "Now, 'Smart' Credit Cards"
   David E. Sange

Newsday

7. May 6, 1984
   "Crime Pays—With Bogus Checks, Fake Credit Cards"
   James D. Diamond

USA Today

8. June 3, 1983
   "Credit Card Fakes: $40M and Growing"
   Carolyn Pesce

Other Publications

The American Bakers' Association

9. "Unless You Have Money to Burn: Remember, Forgers' Credentials May Be Forgeries"

Food Marketing Institute

10. "Food Marketing Institute Supermarket Security Manual"
    Charles I. Miller
    Produced in Cooperation with Miller Brewing Company, 1985

Money Management Institute of Household International

11. "Credit Card Fraud Increases," Spring, 1985

Oklahoma Retail Grocer's Associates

12. "Counterfeit Money Guide: Learn to Recognize These Important Features," 1986

United States Department of Justice

13. "Sourcebook of Criminal Justice Statistics—1985"
    Timothy J. Flanagan and Edmund F. McGarrell, Editors
    Bureau of Justice Statistics
    Washington, D.C.: United States Government Printing Office, 1986

United States Department of the Treasury: U. S. Secret Service

14. "Counterfeiting and Forgery"
15. "The Detection of Counterfeit Currency: A Law Enforcement Officer's Guide"

United States Postal Inspection Service

16. "Check Cashing Precautions"
Notice 178, April 1, 1981

CHAPTER 11

Books

1. Applied Foodservice Sanitation
3rd Edition
Educational Foundation of the National Restaurant Association
John Wiley & Sons, Inc., 1974, 1978, 1985
2. Bar and Beverage Management
David K. Hayes, Ph.D. and Jack D. Ninemeier (consulting authors)
Published for the Cornell University Home Study Program Foodservice Management Series
Chain Store Publishing Company, 1987
3. Food Store Security
Edited by Len Daykin
Prepared for Cornell University Home Study Program
Progressive Grocer, 1981
4. Foodservice Operations Manual: A Guide for Hotels, Restaurants, and Institutions
John C. Birchwood
CBI Books, published by Van Nostrand Reinhold Company, 1979
5. How to Protect Your Business
The Council of Better Business Bureaus
The Benjamin Book Company in association with Prentice-Hall, Inc., 1985
6. Management of Hospitality Operations
Bruce H. Axler
Bobbs-Merrill Company, Inc., 1976
7. Purchasing: Selection and Procurement for the Hospitality Industry
John M. Stephanelli
John Wiley & Sons, Inc., 1981

8. Restaurant Purchasing
   Hugh J. Kelley
   Lebhar-Friedman Books—Chain Store Publishing Corporation,
   1976, 1985

Newspapers and Magazines

Briefing

9. July/August, 1981
   "Petty Thievery by Customers"

Chuck Miller's Loss Prevention Letter for Supermarket Executives

10. October, 1985, Volume 2, Number 10
    "Special Fire Prevention Issue—Pre-fire Plan for Stores"
11. November, 1986, Volume 9, Number 11
    "Protecting the Bottom Line—Product Tampering: Basic Planning
    Reduces Problems"
    Charles I. Miller

Foodservice Marketing

12. June, 1981
    "Security: How You Can Reduce the Risk of Crime in Your
    Restaurant"
    Frederick H. Rice

National Restaurant Association News

13. August, 1984, Volume 4, Number 7
    "What Patrons Pick to Pocket"
    Carole Sugarman
    An excerpted article originally appearing in The Washington Post,
    May 22, 1983

Nation's Restaurant News

14. March 10. 1986
    "Viewpoint: Safety Measures May Avert Tragedy Over Food
    Tampering"
    Ken Rankin
15. April 7, 1986
    "Stiff Extortion Penalty Sought—Atlanta Man Threatens to Taint
    Food Supply"

Restaurants & Institutions

16. December 10, 1986
"Security: Baskin-Robbin's Security System Removes
Temptation"
Lisa Bertagnoli

The Wall Street Journal

17. July 16, 1986
"Food Packaging May Be Improved, but Tampering Can't Be
Prevented"
Trish Hall

Other Publications

Federal Bureau of Investigation

18. "Crime in the United States"
Uniform Crime Reports for the United States, 1985

Food Marketing Institute

19. "Food Marketing Institute Supermarket Security Manual"
Produced in Cooperation with Miller Brewing Company
Researched and written by Charles I. Miller, 1985

Loss Prevention Systems, Inc.

20. 1985
"In-Store Security: Methods and Procedures for Observing . . .
Apprehending . . . Questioning Shoplifters"
Written and presented by Charles I. Miller
NOPA Retail Branch Stores Forum, 1985 Mid-Winter Conference,
Scottsdale, Arizona

United States Department of Justice

21. "Sourcebook of Criminal Justice Statistics—1985"
Timothy J. Flanagan and Edmund F. McGarrell, Editors
Bureau of Justice Statistics
Washington, D.C.: United States Government Printing Office, 1986

CHAPTER 12

Books

1. How to Protect Your Business
   Council of Better Business Bureaus

Newspapers and Magazines

National Restaurant Association News

2. August, 1984
   "Computer Fraud: Practical Steps to Protect Your Computer"
   Bob Hill

Index